LEGACIES OF LIGHT

Modern Heroes of the Christian Faith

Stephen Davey

STEPHEN DAVEY

LEGACIES OF LIGHT

MODERN HEROES OF THE FAITH

CONTENTS

Title Page
Copyright
Preface ... 1
David and Svea Flood ... 3
Amy Carmichael ... 15
A. W. Tozer ... 28
Susanna Wesley ... 41
Oswald Chambers ... 55
Adoniram Judson ... 69
Fanny Crosby ... 83
Jim and Elisabeth Elliot ... 95
Hudson Taylor ... 105
John Newton ... 117
Charles Spurgeon ... 131
George Mueller ... 146
William Cowper ... 157
Katharina Luther ... 170
E. V. Hill and S. M. Lockridge ... 183
Dr. Viggo Olsen ... 193
Endnotes ... 206

Author: Stephen Davey
Editor: Jarl K. Waggoner
Cover Design and Body Layout: Kristin Preston
Sketches by Adam Dohrmann

© 2019 Stephen Davey. All rights reserved.

Unless otherwise noted, all Scripture quotations are from the New American Standard Bible® (NASB),
© 1960, 1962, 1963, 1968, 1971, 1972, 1973, 1975, 1977, 1995 by the Lockman Foundation. Used by permission. www.Lockman.org

Scripture quotations marked MSG are from *The Message*. Copyright © by Eugene H. Peterson 1993, 1994, 1995, 1996, 2000, 2001, 2002. Used by permission of Tyndale House Publishers, Inc.

Scripture quotations marked KJV are from the King James Version of the Bible.

Published by Charity House Publishers

Charity House Publishers, Inc.
2703 Jones Franklin Road
Suite 105
Cary, NC 27518
USA

www.wisdomonline.org

PREFACE

The Word of God is filled with biographical details, as one character after another parades across the stage of redemptive history. These patriarchs, prophets, judges, apostles, and faithful followers of the Lord fill key roles in furthering God's eternal plan. Yet they also serve another purpose: they teach us lessons by the lives they lived.

The New Testament writers often repeated the challenge to the early believers to imitate the faith, actions, and attitudes of godly individuals past and present. Those first readers of the New Testament learned how to follow and serve Christ, not only from the instructions of the apostolic authors but also from observing how the truths the apostles taught were lived out in the lives of other Christians. Paul told Titus and Timothy to be good examples worthy of imitation (Titus 2:7; 1 Timothy 4:12). He even held himself forth as an example to other believers, inasmuch as he imitated Christ (1 Corinthians 11:1; Philippians 3:17).

The great American poet Henry Wadsworth Longfellow put this challenge to rhyme in his 1838 poem "A Psalm of Life," when he wrote:

Lives of great men all remind us...

We can make our lives sublime,

And, departing, leave behind us

Footprints on the sands of time.

It is quite obvious that God loves to teach lasting lessons

through the lives of individuals. With that in mind, the biographical sketches presented in this book illustrate biblical truths through the lives of believers ranging from the sixteenth to the twenty-first centuries—men and women who provide for us wonderful legacies of light.

DAVID AND SVEA FLOOD

In the early 1800s, a Presbyterian minister named Robert Murray McCheyne pastored a church in Scotland—ever so briefly.

He served in what we would call a pastor/teacher role for less than five years, but in that time he saw some seven hundred people come to faith in Jesus Christ. He used to tell other pastors, "Preach to your people as on the brink of eternity."

Robert died from typhus at the age of twenty-nine. Yet his ministry was so profoundly effective that Scotland was impacted for decades to come, and even today, almost two hundred years later, his life is the subject of study and he is held in great esteem.

John Philips wrote that several years after Robert McCheyne's death, another pastor was deeply concerned that his own ministry was producing so little spiritual fruit, and he decided to visit the church where McCheyne had pastored. He found a custodian busily at work and asked him if he could show him around, and the man did. The pastor asked this humble man if he knew the secret to McCheyne's fruitful ministry. The old man led the young minister into McCheyne's study and said, "Sit down there at that desk. Now, put your elbows on the table." He did so. "Yes, that was the way McCheyne used to do it," said the old man. "Now, put your face in your hands." The visitor obeyed. "Now, let the tears run down your cheeks. That was what McCheyne used to do."[1]

Sowing in Tears

The psalmist wrote, "Those who sow in tears shall reap with joyful shouting. He who goes to and fro weeping, carrying his bag of seed, shall indeed come again with a shout of joy, bringing his sheaves with him" (Psalm 126:5-6).

While the immediate context is the return of Israel from

exile, the concept of sowing and bearing fruit was picked up and applied by our Lord when He talked about the seed of the Word of God (Matthew 13:3-9, 18-23). Paul likewise used the same analogy when he referred to planting the seed and God making it grow (1 Corinthians 3:6).

And in the case of both Jesus and Paul, their sacrificial labors were accompanied by tears. Paul told the Corinthians that his letters were bathed in tears (2 Corinthians 2:4). And he reminded the Ephesian elders that he had taught them "with tears and with trials" (Acts 20:19).

The Bible records that Jesus, too, shed tears.

In John 11, Jesus arrived at the tomb of His friend Lazarus, who had been dead for four days. Verse 33 tells us, "When Jesus therefore saw her [Mary, Lazarus's sister] weeping, and the Jews who had come with her also weeping, He was deeply moved in his spirit and was troubled."

In other words, Jesus was moved deeply when he saw the grief and heard the weeping brought about by death. And then verse 35 tells us simply, "Jesus wept." He shared the grief that death brings, even though He knew the tears would be followed by joy and a harvest of resurrection power as He raised Lazarus to life.

Hebrews 5:7 says, "In the days of His flesh, He offered up both prayers and supplications with loud crying and tears to the One able to save Him from death."

No doubt Jesus wept on numerous occasions. We know He lamented, or cried, over His nation in Matthew 23:37, saying, "Jerusalem, Jerusalem . . . I wanted to gather your children together, the way a hen gathers her chicks under her wings, and you were unwilling."

Hebrews 5:7, however, is an inside look at the garden of Gethsemane, where Jesus wept as He anticipated His coming substitutionary death for the sins of the world. He surrendered to the will of the Father, with much crying and in great agony, signifying His willingness to die.

Jesus came to the garden with His disciples and told them, "Sit here while I go over there and pray" (Matthew 26:36).

Jesus then "took with Him Peter and the two sons of Zebedee [James and John], and began to be grieved and distressed" (verse 37). The word "distressed" describes intense sorrow and discomfort.

Then He said to them, "My soul is deeply grieved, to the point of death; remain here and keep watch with Me" (verse 38).

Why was Jesus so "deeply grieved" and desirous of His disciples' presence with Him?

- Was He troubled over their coming desertion of Him and Peter's denials?
- Was He grieved and sorrowful over His nation's rejection of Him? Were the words already ringing in His ears: "Crucify Him! . . . We have no king but Caesar" (John 19:15)?
- Was He dreading the coming pain of crucifixion?
- Was it the ugly truth that He would become sin for us, when He had never known one single sin?
- Was He weeping over the coming loss of fellowship with the Father as He suffered the penalty of humanity's sin?

Probably all of the above are involved.

There in the garden Jesus Christ wept in deep grief, but what a difference Sunday morning would bring! Like a seed, isolated, dying, and buried, His death would be translated into a harvest of joy.

The seed of self-sacrifice sown with tears ultimately produces a joyful harvest. This truth has been demonstrated a thousand times over in the lives of believers. Those who were surrounded by the sorrow of night have seen the tables turned—though for some it came only after they died—and then the sorrow of night was replaced with joy that came in the morning.

A Christian couple from Sweden provide one of the most touching demonstrations of self-sacrifice, death, tears, sorrow... and fruit.

The Seed of Self-sacrifice

In 1921 David Flood, his young wife, Svea, and their little two-year-old son left Sweden for the interior of Africa. They traveled with another young missionary couple, the Ericksons. These two couples were active church members; they sang in the choir, and Svea played the violin and was the church soloist. But they had committed their lives to taking the gospel to unreached tribes in Africa.

They were filled with enthusiasm and optimism as they literally hacked their way through the mountains of the Congo, eager to begin their ministry at some yet undetermined, unreached village. To their surprise, however, one village after another refused them entrance, convinced that they would anger the village gods and bring great trouble upon the people.

After days of carrying their own supplies, they were hungry and weak. They prayed as they reached another village on the side of a mountain that they would finally find rest and ministry opportunities. But the chief in the village was even more hostile than all the others. He demanded that they leave.

They carried their supplies farther up the mountain and put up their tents. They were too weary to set out again, so they decided to clear the brush and build mud huts and do their best to reach these hostile villagers.

During the next agonizing weeks, which stretched into agonizing months, David and Svea Flood struggled with learning Swahili and, along with the Ericksons, tried everything they could to reach out to the villagers below. The village chief only tightened his grip on his people.

The people were prohibited from even visiting the missionaries, except for one little boy who was allowed to go up and sell them chickens and eggs.

David was amazed at his wife's insistence that while they might never reach the village—and probably never impact Africa—she could perhaps win this child for Jesus Christ. Every time this boy visited their camp, she showered him with love and attention, and, sure enough, one afternoon the other missionaries watched as Svea knelt with this little boy and led him in a prayer of repentance. The boy had to keep his decision for Christ a secret in the village, lest he not be allowed to return, or worse.

Eventually the Ericksons decided to leave David, Svea, and their little boy and return to an established mission station many miles away. Even though the Flood family battled malaria and desperately crude conditions, they decided to stay.

Sometime later Svea announced that she was expecting their second child. She was already weak and struggling physically, and David feared the worst.

It was too late to travel through the jungles of the Belgian Congo without risking her life and the life of their unborn child. The baby would be born in their mud hut, on the mountain. The newly converted boy carried the news back to the village, and the chief surprisingly allowed one of the women to serve as a midwife.

By the time the baby was due, Svea Flood was weak with malaria. When the African midwife arrived, Svea was groaning in pain and suffering from high fever.

When the little girl was born, Svea whispered that she was to be called Aina (ah-ee-nah), a classic name for Swedish girls. Seventeen days later, Svea Flood died.

Hopeless and filled with bitter rage, David dug a crude grave for his twenty-seven-year-old wife. How could he possibly care for his young son, plus a sickly little baby girl, without assistance?

He hired a young man from the village, along with several others, and took his children down the mountain and to the mission station. He was finished with the ministry, the gospel, and God. As far as he was concerned, God had taken the life of his faithful bride and their ministry had been nothing less than a tragic waste.

Returning to Sweden was a monumental task for David. He knew that he had no one to feed or care for his baby girl.

The Ericksons had been unable to have children, so David offered them the opportunity to adopt Aina. They were thrilled at the chance and agreed to do so.

With that, David took his son and left the station, never to return again. He never even looked back.

Before Aina turned one year old, Joel and Bertha Erickson's food was poisoned by unbelieving natives. They died within days of each other.

Aina was once again without parents, but she was soon claimed by another missionary couple and raised as their own daughter. When she was three years old, Aina and her adoptive parents left the mission field of Africa for good and eventually settled in South Dakota. Her Swedish name was changed to

Aggie.

Aggie would later write that even as a young girl, she knew she was different. She would become known as the daughter of the missionary who died on the mountain, rescued by missionaries who were poisoned, and, as her biography title says, she would become a girl without a country.[2]

A Joyful Harvest

Eventually, Aggie attended North Central Bible College in Minneapolis and married a godly young man who entered the ministry.

Years went by. Aggie had no information about her father and knew very little of her past. She knew her parents' names, of course, and that their homeland was Sweden, but that was about it.

She hardly had time to think about it—with a husband and a family and a busy ministry. Her husband, Dewey Hurst, had become president of a Bible college in Seattle, Washington.

Then one day, unexpectedly, a Swedish religious magazine appeared in her mailbox. She had no idea who had sent it, and she couldn't read the words. But as she turned the pages, one photograph arrested her attention. It was a picture of a small white cross planted in the earth over an obvious burial site—and on the cross was the name Svea Flood.

She immediately took the magazine to a college professor who could translate the article. The professor translated as she read, telling how two missionaries pushing through the African jungle, camping at night and traveling by day, came across a village in the Belgian Congo and found the burial plot they had photographed.

They began to inquire and found out that this was the grave of a missionary who had died shortly after giving birth to a baby girl, but not before leading one African boy to Christ. The woman's widowed husband had left their daughter in the hands of fellow missionaries.

The article continued, saying that, sadly, Svea Flood didn't live long enough to learn that the little African boy they had won to Christ on that mountaintop in time went on to gain permission from the village chief to start and build a school.

Gradually, this now mature young man, teacher, and leader, taught the gospel of Christ, and all his students came to trust in Jesus Christ as well. They then evangelized their parents, and even the chief became a Christian. Now that village had six hundred believers and an active church professing Jesus Christ as Lord and Savior.

All this came from the sacrifice and the tears and the sowing of David and, primarily, Svea Flood.

Aggie couldn't believe the news. She began to cry and thank God for letting her learn the truth of her parents and their sacrifice and the harvest of fruit.

For their twenty-fifth wedding anniversary, the Bible college gave the Hursts a vacation to Sweden, where, among other things, Aggie could search for her father.

It wasn't difficult to find his family. David Flood had remarried and had four more children before his second wife also died. Now, an old man, he was wasting away as an alcoholic and professed agnostic who dared anyone to talk to him about God.

After a joyous meeting with her half brothers and half sister, Aggie brought up the subject of seeing their father. Her siblings weren't too optimistic about the idea. Their father had become deeply bitter, had little to do with any of them, and, most of all, hated God. They warned her that whenever he heard the name of God, he flew into a rage.

Aggie was determined to see him. She eventually made it to his little apartment, where the door was answered by a housekeeper. Inside his room there were liquor bottles on every window sill; the table was covered with more bottles. And in the far corner was a small, wrinkled old man lying on a rumpled bed, his head turned away.

Diabetes and a stroke had confined him to this one room for the past three years.

"Papa?" she said tentatively.

He turned and began to cry. "Aina" he said, "I never meant to give you away."

"It's all right, Papa," she replied, taking him gently in her arms. "God took care of me."

The man instantly stiffened. The tears stopped.

"God forgot all of us. Our lives have been like this because of Him." He turned his face back to the wall.

Aggie stroked his face and then continued, undaunted.

"Papa, I've got a little story to tell you, and it's a true one. You didn't go to Africa in vain. Mama didn't die in vain. The little boy you won to the Lord grew up to win that whole village to Jesus Christ. The one seed you planted just kept growing and growing. Today there are six hundred African people serving the Lord because you were faithful to the call of God in your life.... Papa, Jesus loves you. He has never hated you."

The old man turned back to look into his daughter's eyes. His body relaxed. He began to talk. And by the end of the afternoon, he had come back to the God he had resented for so many decades.

Over the next few days, father and daughter enjoyed warm moments together. Aggie and her husband soon had to return to America—and within a few weeks, David Flood had gone into eternity.[3]

Let me give you an addendum to this remarkable story.

A few years later Aggie and her husband attended an evangelism conference in London. A report was given from the nation of Zaire (formerly the Belgian Congo) by the superintendent of the national church association; he represented over 100,000 baptized believers. He spoke of the amazing spread of the gospel in his nation.

Afterward, Aggie rushed forward to ask him if he had ever heard of her parents, David and Svea Flood.

"Yes madam," the man replied in French, his words then being translated into English. "It was Svea Flood who led me to Jesus Christ. I was the boy who brought food to your parents before you were born. In fact, to this day your mother's grave and her memory are honored by all of us."

He embraced her in a long, sobbing hug. Then he continued, "You must come to Africa to see, because your mother is the most famous person in our history."[4]

She agreed, and after months of planning, Aggie and her husband made the long journey back to the place of her birth.

They eventually arrived at the outpost where she had been given by her father to the Ericksons. This was the outpost where she had lived as a little toddler, playing in the dirt with her African friends, learning the Swahili language. There she visited the graves of her first adoptive parents.

Then they drove several miles to the village her parents

had desperately tried to reach. Only this time, there were hundreds of villagers waiting and cheering as she came into view—they had built arches covered with flowers for her reception.

Eventually, the pastor of the village church took her up the hill to a flat place beneath a grove of trees. This was where her parents' mud house once stood . . . this was where she was born.

He then pointed her to a simple grave overlooking the valley below. Marking the grave was that small white cross, and on it was written, "Svea Flood (1896-1923)." Aggie was standing where her mother had stood, declaring the gospel to one small boy. Now she knew the harvest of the seed her mother had sown.

Later, in the church, with believing villagers crowding around, the pastor read the words of Psalm 126:5: "Those who sow in tears shall reap with joyful shouting."[5]

God knows what it means to weep. God knows what it means to suffer loss. God knows what it means to sow seed that doesn't seem to bear fruit.

But God also knows the end. He knows that tears of sorrow, loss, frustration, pain, and grief will soon be wiped away—replaced by indescribable joy.

And the fruit of His gospel seed—you and me and the fruit of our efforts (the extent of which we may not even know), along with David and Svea Flood and hundreds of African villagers, and millions of others, all the fruit of His harvest—will live forever.

AMY CARMICHAEL

In 1867, the first of seven children was born into an Irish family known as the Carmichaels. Although David and Catherine Carmichael were dedicated Christians, they had no idea that their firstborn, Amy, would grow up to become one of the modern world's most revered missionaries.

What they learned very quickly, however, was that Amy was strong-willed and rather hard to handle. As a little girl she was even nicknamed Wild Irish. Whenever there was mischief in the Carmichael household, Amy was usually the instigator.

Her determined will and fiery personality were displayed when she was around five years old. Her mother had told her that if she would pray about her needs, God would answer her prayer. Amy had brown eyes, which she felt would be much better if they were Irish blue. And so one night she prayed that God would change the color of her eyes to blue. The next morning, she jumped out of bed and ran to the mirror. Mrs. Carmichael could hear Amy wailing in frustration and disappointment. She had trouble explaining to her daughter that God sometimes answers prayers by saying no, and He always has a reason for doing so, even if Amy didn't like it.[6]

Only years later did she recognize why God had given her brown eyes instead of blue: they allowed her to effectively impersonate a native Indian woman so that she could enter a Hindu temple unsuspected and sneak away a young girl who was being kept as a prostitute—literally a sex slave—by the Brahmin priests.

On another occasion, an adult told young Amy that she needed to stop swallowing prune seeds because if she didn't, she would grow plum trees out of her head. Amy promptly swallowed twelve of them, delighted with the idea of growing an orchard on her head.

This sense of strong determination would serve her well years later in India when she abandoned the European dress for Indian attire, eventually dropped her English mission agency and created her own, and bucked the caste system of India, building an orphanage and treating all the staff and children equally.

Turning Points

At the age of fifteen, Amy believed the gospel and placed her life in the hands of God the Father through faith in Jesus Christ.

One Sunday morning two years later, Amy was walking home from a church service with her mother and brothers when they met a woman—one we might call a street person—burdened down with a heavy load of rags. Instantly, Amy and her brothers relieved the woman of her bundle, took her arms, and helped her along. Amy remembered the icy stares of the other church members, whom she called "proper Presbyterians." They obviously disapproved of their actions. You just didn't get your hands dirty like that.

Amy would later write that as she helped that old woman with her bundle of rags, some verses of Scripture flashed into her mind. They would become life verses for her.

> *For no man can lay a foundation other than the one which is laid, which is Jesus Christ. Now if any man builds on the foundation with gold, silver, precious stones, wood, hay, straw, each man's work will become evident; for the day will show it because it is to be revealed with fire, and the fire itself will test the quality of each*

man's work. (1 Corinthians 3:11-13)

In this text, the apostle references the coming evaluation of every Christian's life. This isn't a time of punishment but a time of reward.

Paul expounds further on this judgment, which we call the judgment seat of Christ, in 2 Corinthians:

Therefore we also have as our ambition, whether at home or absent, to be pleasing to Him. For we must all appear before the judgment seat of Christ, so that each one may be recompensed for his deeds in the body. (2 Corinthians 5:9-10)

Now we're clearly told that no one is saved by good works. Ephesians 2:8-9 says, "For by grace you have been saved through faith; and that not of yourselves, it is the gift of God; not as a result of works, so that no one may boast."

However, even though salvation isn't *earned* by good works, it is definitely *evidenced* by good works. As the Reformers put it so well centuries ago, saving faith is faith in Christ alone, but saving faith is never alone.

In other words, genuine faith is accompanied by good works that glorify the Father and cause the world to both see and hear the gospel. So, what are we revealing with our lives?

First Corinthians 3:11-13 is one of those passages that challenge the Christian to live a godly, passionate, disciplined, intentional life. It's a call to offer our best to God.

What are we giving to God? Is it empty works that will burn up under the gaze of Christ? Or do we offer Him that which will last?

We should note, too, that Paul makes it clear in this text that our Christian service for Christ is not a matter of quantity but of quality. That's Paul's challenge to the believer here: do we offer Christ precious gems or cheap straw? Are we giving Him the leftovers we can do without or costly gifts?

It was this passage that sent Amy Carmichael to her room that afternoon when she came home from helping the woman on the street. She prayed in anguish over the thought that she might settle for the religious status quo, that she might keep her hands from getting dirty in the ministry of the gospel, that her life might make so little difference in people's lives and for God's glory. This day—and this passage—would echo throughout the rest of her life.[7]

God would soon test her resolve.

Not long after this signature event, Amy's father died unexpectedly, and the family's financial security was suddenly gone. Eventually, Amy moved into the home of a godly widower. He was the cofounder of the Keswick Convention, and Amy would serve as his secretary for several years. The Keswick movement emphasized victorious Christian living through the power of the Holy Spirit.

Beginnings in Missions

By this time, the Lord had already burdened her heart for young women who worked in a nearby mill. They were nicknamed Shawlies because they were too poor to purchase hats and so they wore shawls, pulled up around their heads. Her ministry among these women was very effective, and in a matter of months, a number of young women had trusted Christ as their Lord and Savior.

Living in the home of the Keswick leader allowed Amy the privilege of meeting choice servants of God like F. B. Meyer and Hudson Taylor. Amy soon began to sense the Lord directing her to leave her local ministry for some distant land.

Jesus' words in Mark 16:15 took hold of her: "Go ye into all the world, and preach the gospel to every creature" (KJV). She would write that these words began to play over and over in her heart and mind: "Go ye ... Go ye ... Go ye."

In the original language, this is an imperative, a command: "Go, you," or "You, go." Jesus was saying, "You go, and deliver the gospel to the nations—not someone else but you!"

About that same time, Amy heard Hudson Taylor preach. He spoke of unbelieving Chinese dying at the rate of one million a month. That further arrested her thinking. Mark 16:15 became her personal call from Christ to leave her homeland of Great Britain—to leave what she called the "luxury of light" and go into the darkness.

Amy applied to Hudson Taylor's China Inland Mission, but she was rejected because of her poor health. In fact, she was not healthy. She suffered from neuralgia, pain that extends along the path of the nerves. This led to weakness and persistent illness. Often she was forced to lie in bed for weeks at a time.

Undeterred by the rejection, a year later Amy was on a ship heading for Japan as a missionary. She served there little more than a year and returned home, her health broken.

For most people that would have been enough. She could have been satisfied with her commendable effort and with her sacrifice and willingness to go. But not this wild Irishwoman who once dreamed of growing an orchard on her head. She knew God had called her to some distant and darkened culture. She wanted to do something for God that no one had done before!

Amy would later write, "Satan is so much more in earnest than we are—he buys up the opportunity while we are wondering how much it will cost us."

Work in India

To the surprise of everyone and the concern of many, Amy set sail for India just a year later, this time with a different mission board under the Church of England. India was not exactly an easier place to serve. A number of sources indicate that even the missionaries who greeted her in India predicted she would not last six months on the field.

In fact, Amy struggled with poor health and with loneliness. She also struggled to learn the Tamil language, which would enable her to share the gospel with those around her. Yet Amy Carmichael would end up serving in India for fifty-five years—and without ever returning home on furlough.

Her ministry, however, would take a turn she never expected. It would result in misunderstandings from her supporting church, disagreements with other missionaries, an angry power play by an influential family in England in an attempt to stop her work, and trouble with the law of the land. But Amy would choose to stay, create her own mission agency, and trust Christ to keep her out of prison and take care of her financial needs.

It all began with a little girl name Preena.

When she was just seven years old, Preena's parents sold her to the local Hindu temple, where she supposedly was married to the gods. In reality she was inducted into a world that today goes by the name sex trafficking. Sadly, in her day and in that culture, this evil was accepted and even revered.

The practice had begun in the sixth century. Young girls were sold by their parents to the Hindu priests, who taught them to sing and dance. When they reached puberty, they would be forced into lives of inescapable tragedy. They were nothing more than slaves of the Brahmin priests, used and abused by the men who came to the temple with their gifts of money and food.

When Preena realized what her life would actually become, she escaped and eventually made her way back to her home, where she thought she would be safe. But no sooner had she reached home than a woman from the temple arrived as well, demanding that Preena be given back immediately.

Amy wrote that Preena's arms were clutching her mother's waist as she cried to be rescued. The woman from the temple warned that the Hindu gods would bring down their wrath upon the family if they did not give up their daughter. Fearing the Hindu deities, Preena's mother actually unloosed her daughter's clinging arms and handed her over to the woman.

When she was returned to the temple, the priests took hot irons and branded Preena's hands as punishment.[8] Preena refused to give up, however. Soon, she ran away again. This time she made her way to a nearby village, where a Christian woman found her and hid her.

It happened, by the providence of God, Amy Carmichael was visiting that very village that afternoon. When she met Preena and heard her story, Amy uncovered an ugly sore on Mother India's body—fathers and mothers were selling their daughters to various gods, turning their precious daughters into temple prostitutes.

Amy went into action.

A village in southern India called Dohnavur became her mission headquarters. Soon built on about one hundred acres of land were a school, a home, a hospital, and an orphanage. But primarily it was a refuge that Amy nicknamed "The Gray Jungle Retreat."

It wasn't long before seventeen young girls had escaped or been rescued from nearby temples and brought to the sanctuary at Dohnavur. The children all called Amy, Amma, which means "mother." Eventually her haven at Dohnavur cared for little boys and abandoned babies as well. They all called her Amma.

Interestingly, most of the children who came to this refuge did not know their birthdate. So, they chose as their birthday the day they arrived at Amy Carmichael's mission. They called it their "coming day." They celebrated that day as their birthday because on that day they began to finally live.

In her work, Amy faced much opposition. She was often accused of kidnapping, but she faced her accusers without backing down. Amazingly, many missionaries were appalled that Amy would interrupt the caste system and even dare to whisk little girls away in the night from Hindu temples.

She wrote about her experiences for her supporters back home, but one book manuscript she hoped would open the eyes of her countrymen was refused by the publisher, who sent it back for revision, saying it was too discouraging. She refused to alter it and later published it under the title *Things as They Are*.

A Lasting Legacy

Amy pressed on, sacrificing all she had—gold, silver, and precious stones—for the gospel of Christ.

Over the decades, without ever seeking it, Amy Carmichael began to gain international acclaim. The queen of England provided funds for a hospital at Dohnavur, and mission agencies sent her requests to come and speak.

At the height of her growing fame, Amy was walking through the compound one night, unaware that workers had dug a large pit. She fell into the pit, breaking her leg and twisting her spine in the fall. The injury would leave her largely bedridden for the last twenty years of her life.

She wrote in her journal, "We are not asked to understand, but simply to obey."

Those twenty bedridden years turned out to be amazingly profitable. Amy wrote a half-dozen books, along with poetry, that inspired thousands of people to make their lives count for Christ—to accept the personal call to go and build a life with precious jewels and costly sacrifices, a life that pleases the Lord.

In a wonderful book that introduced me to Amy Carmichael's missionary work, Warren Wiersbe asked an honest question: What church today would support a missionary like Amy Carmichael?

Consider these facts:

- She spent nearly sixty years on the mission field and never once came home to report to her supporters.
- She went to the field under the authority of a mission board but pretty much did her own thing, upsetting conventional norms, ignoring the caste system, dressing like an Indian woman, and demanding that everyone in her mission go by his or her Indian name.
- She left her mission board and started an organization on her own.
- She went to the field to carry on one kind of ministry but within a few years began an entirely different ministry that got her into trouble with the law. In fact, on one occasion she faced a seven-year prison sentence for "assisting in the kidnapping of a child." (The case was later dropped.)
- The reports she mailed home were often too strange to be believed—or too shocking.
- She was asked repeatedly to return home for a visit, but she refused to leave her mission. She said she didn't have time and wouldn't fly in one of those airplanes anyway because, as she explained, the devil is the prince of the power of the air, and she had no desire

to fly through his territory. (That's certainly a strange view to us, but many in her generation felt the same way.)
- The final twenty years of her ministry, she was practically an invalid, directing the work from her bedroom.[9]

Indeed, who would support a missionary like that?

Amy Carmichael was stubborn and strong-willed to the end; in fact, when she was eighty years old, she read a reviewer's comment that her books were popular. "Popular?" she responded. "Lord, is that what these books written out of the heat of battle are to people? Popular? O Lord, burn my books to ashes if that is true."[10]

She wrote to aspiring missionary candidates with honest realism, telling them they would never make it in India as a missionary unless they brought with them a sense of humor and absolutely no sense of smell. She would tell other candidates that above everything else, serving with her offered them one thing only: a chance to die.

Amy lived up to her life verses, which tell us that God desires to see in us the most precious sacrifices, not so we can be saved, but so we can bring glory to the God who saved us and then called us to go. Is it not ironic that so many children found a home because she was willing to give up hers?

When Amy died in 1951 at the age of eighty-three, she left behind a magnificent legacy—the precious, priceless lives of hundreds of children whose lives were physically and spiritually rescued by the gospel. That legacy was built upon the foundation of Christ.

As death neared, Amy Carmichael insisted that no grave marker be placed where she was buried. She wanted no temptation left to her teammates to build some shrine in her honor.

They honored her wish—to a point. On top of her grave they placed a birdbath bearing a simple plaque with one word engraved on it: Amma.

She lived more than sixty years anticipating the day when she will be evaluated and rewarded for the true quality of her life, a life lived with authenticity, integrity, truth, humility, perseverance, love, and faith.

This is what the apostle Paul meant when he wrote of a life built upon the foundation of Christ with priceless deeds of gold and silver and precious stones. This is the life of one willing to be sacrificed, to face the penalties, to embrace the costs of being a disciple of Jesus Christ.

I close with the words to a poem Amy Carmichael wrote. It reveals her attitude toward life, ministry, and suffering. It reveals the life she wanted, a life that mattered, a life devoted to following Jesus Christ.

> From prayer that asks that I may be
> Sheltered from winds that beat on Thee,
> From fearing when I should aspire,
> From faltering when I should climb higher,
> From silken self, O Captain, free
> Thy soldier who would follow Thee.
>
> From subtle love of softening things,
> From easy choices, weakenings,
> (Not thus are spirits fortified,
> Not this way went the Crucified,)
> From all that dims Thy Calvary
> O Lamb of God, deliver me.

Give me the love that leads the way,
The faith that nothing can dismay
The hope no disappointments tire,
The passion that will burn like fire;
Let me not sink to be a clod;
Make me Thy fuel, Oh Flame of God.[11]

A. W. TOZER

On the day of Pentecost, the apostle Peter stood up in Jerusalem and delivered the sermon that effectively launched the New Testament church. In the midst of his sermon, he also gave an invitation—the first of its kind to be applied to New Testament Christianity. It was a quote from the prophet Joel: "And it shall be that everyone who calls on the name of the Lord will be saved" (Acts 2:21).

We aren't given the full manuscript of Peter's sermon. Luke, the writer of the book of Acts, simply says that "with many other words" Peter kept on exhorting his audience to "be saved [literally, rescued] from this perverse [unbelieving] generation" (Acts 2:40).

Luke goes on to add that three thousand people believed the gospel Peter proclaimed in his sermon (Acts 2:41); namely, that the Man they had crucified had risen from the dead and was none other than the anointed, sovereign Lord (Acts 2:36). They accepted the invitation. In faith they called upon the name of the Lord and were saved.

That same gospel invitation would be acted upon some 1,900 years later in the heart and life of a farm boy named Aiden Wilson Tozer.

Aiden was born in 1897 in a small farming community in western Pennsylvania. His family was extremely poor and struggled to make ends meet.

When Aiden was fifteen years old, the Tozer family moved to Akron, Ohio, and landed jobs in the automobile tire industry. One afternoon in 1912, as Aiden was walking home from his job at Goodyear, he overhead a street preacher exhorting a crowd to call on the Lord in order to be saved.

Tozer knew the gospel, and at that moment, the Spirit of God convicted his heart. He went home and immediately climbed up into the attic, where he fell to his knees and called upon God to save him.

He knew immediately that he was different. In fact, he knew intuitively that Christians were different from everyone else. He would later write, "A Real Christian is an odd number anyway. He feels supreme love for One he has never seen, talks familiarly every day to Someone he cannot see, expects to go to heaven on the virtue of Another."[12]

Passion for Ministry

And so, A. W. Tozer's Christian life began. And he would soon discover that he was not only out of step with his world but also out of step with the opinions and lifestyles of the Christian world at large.

His ministry as a prophetic voice began in earnest seven years later. Then, at the age of twenty-two and without any formal training, he began forty-four years of pastoral ministry.

Tozer struggled with weak lungs and a voice that he himself said had a nasal quality to it and needed improving. His biographer, James Snyder writes,

> *Typical of Tozer, he went to a bookstore and purchased a volume on voice training to learn all he could about voice control. In his office was a large copy of Milton's Paradise Lost and Tozer would place it on a music stand borrowed from the sanctuary and read it aloud. He would end up reading the book four times in order to strengthen his voice and gain better control. He even carried balloons in his briefcase and blew them up to help strengthen his*

lungs.[13]

It wasn't vanity, however. It was deep-rooted passion to be the best spokesman for God he could possibly be. Indeed, he didn't care what people thought about him. He simply wanted to preach the truth.

In Warren Wiersbe's biographical comments on Tozer, he wrote, "I heard Tozer preach many times—and it was about as safe as opening the door of a furnace."[14]

Tozer would preach anywhere; denominations meant nothing to him. Instead, he would look for what he called the fellowship of burning hearts.

He was also blatantly critical of Christian authors. For instance, he once read a Christian book, after which he commented that it had as much spiritual benefit as shaving with a banana. The author never quite forgave him for that.

Thirty of Tozer's years were spent in Chicago at Southside Alliance Church. He saw the church grow from eighty people to nearly a thousand. He was later elected editor of the Missionary and Alliance magazine, then called the Alliance Weekly. His first article appeared on June 3, 1950.

These articles immediately challenged the status quo within the evangelical church. In fact, in that first editorial, Tozer wrote, "It will cost something to walk slow in the parade of the ages while excited men of time rush about confusing motion with progress. But it will pay in the long run, and the true Christian is not much interested in anything short of that."[15]

Throughout Tozer's forty-four years of ministry, he consistently called the Christian and the church to a new reformation. He constantly warned of spiritual decline.

For instance, he wrote, "Until we have a reformation, all of our books and our schools and our magazines are only the working of bacteria in the decaying Church."[16]

The ministry passion of A. W. Tozer can be summarized by the verses he quoted at the beginning of one of his books:

> *Therefore if you have been raised up with Christ, keep seeking the things above, where Christ is, seated at the right hand of God. Set your mind on the things above, not on the things that are on earth. For you have died and your life is hidden with Christ in God. When Christ, who is our life, is revealed, then you also will be revealed with Him in glory. (Colossians 3:1-4)*

To see Christ exalted, seated, sovereign, to see God as majestic and glorified—that would become A. W. Tozer's driving passion.

He wrote in his book, *The Knowledge of the Holy*,

> *So necessary to the Church is a lofty concept of God that when that concept in any measure declines, the Church with her worship and her moral standards declines along with it. The first step down for any church is taken when it surrenders its high opinion of God. . . . We do the greatest service to the next generation of Christians by passing on to them undimmed and undiminished that noble concept of God.[17]*

Tozer obviously and passionately believed in this exalted vision of Christ to whom every believer is to surrender. He often offended anyone who fell short of that vision. He wrote that so much of what passes for New Testament Christianity is little more than truth sweetened with music, made palatable by religious entertainment.

He was once asked to speak at a holiness church one Sunday morning. Before he spoke, the service was, in his view, filled with nothing less than silly music and other forms of entertainment. When it came time for him to preach, he got up and without any warmth or introduction said, "Whatever happened to the holiness of God to you holiness people?" He then set his sermon aside and proceeded to preach on the holiness of God.[18]

Keep in mind that Tozer was challenging the church of the last generation. Imagine what he'd say to our generation.

To Christians fifty years ago Tozer said, "We have sold out to carnal methods, carnal philosophies, carnal viewpoints, carnal gadgets and have lost the glory of God in our midst.

We're a starved generation that's never seen the glory of God."[19]

If that weren't painful enough to hear, Tozer's criticism could become even sharper. He is commonly reported to have written, "The church today is limping from one gimmick to another like so many drunks in a fog."[20]

No wonder, as an older man, Tozer would say to a friend that he had preached himself off every platform in the country.

But he wasn't all about criticism. Tozer preached and wrote of biblical solutions.

He spoke to his generation and to ours these powerful words:

> *To regain her lost power, the church must have a transforming vision of God—not the utilitarian God who is having a run of popularity today, whose chief claim to men's attention is His ability to bring them success; the God we must learn to know is the Majesty in the heavens; He it is that sits upon the circle of the earth who stretches*

out the heavens as a curtain; who brings out His starry host by number and calls them all by names through the greatness of His power.[21]

Again, A. W. Tozer lived with the desire to see Paul's challenge to the Colossians become a reality in the church, to see Christ as exalted Lord.

In an attempt to summarize Tozer's legacy, I want to point out three aspects of his ministry that continue to demand another hearing as a challenge to and evaluation of the church in *our* generation.

Preaching and Teaching

One of Tozer's greatest legacies relates to the matter of preaching and teaching the Bible. I find his emphasis here particularly challenging and encouraging.

Tozer wrote that the lack of genuine exposition of Scripture is often nothing more than the preacher's unwillingness to get himself into trouble.[22] But Tozer would remind us all that preachers are not diplomats delivering compromises; they are prophets delivering ultimatums.

That's because, as he noted, the purpose of genuine exposition is application; that is, biblical preaching desires nothing less than moral and theological reform. He wrote:

No man is better [off] for knowing that God in the beginning created the heavens and the earth. The devil knows that, and so did Ahab and Judas Iscariot. No man is better for knowing that God so loved the world of men that He gave His only begotten Son to die for their redemption. In hell there are millions who know that. . . . The purpose behind all doctrine [and the preaching of it] is to secure moral action.[23]

Biblical knowledge is not given to us or to be imparted by us simply for the sake of knowledge. In fact, Tozer once shocked his world by writing it this way: "The devil is a better theologian than all of us put together . . . but he has no part in God's kingdom."[24] In other words, with all the knowledge the devil has, which must be incredible, he is still the devil.

As I read through pages and pages of Tozer's comments on the pulpit and the pastorate, it became obvious that he would have little patience with the contemporary preaching of our generation that skips from one verse to another, offering platitude after platitude, while avoiding the hard passages and anything doctrinally divisive. He would rightly view this as essentially encouraging the biblical illiteracy of the church. Likewise, he would not applaud the mere intellectual approach to teaching the Bible that demands no action, no change, no conviction, and no purity.

Tozer issued this warning: "We must not select a few favorite passages to the exclusion of all others; nothing less than a whole Bible can make a whole Christian."[25]

The Value of Music

Another lasting legacy of Tozer is the importance he placed on music. We might not automatically view him as a lover of sacred music, but he was passionate about its value.

While he decried the entertainment aspects he felt had entangled the church, Tozer loved the corporate worship of God through music. But he wanted music that exalted Christ. He often counseled young people to get a hymnbook, but not to get one that was less than a hundred years old.[26]

Throughout his ministry, Tozer risked offending those

within his denomination by refusing to use the Missionary and Alliance hymnal. He chose instead to fill his church pews with an old version of a Brethren hymnal "because it contained those great hymns of the faith."[27]

Tozer simply understood, like the Reformers of old, the value of theologically sound music. He put it this way: "Let any young Christian spend a year prayerfully meditating on the hymns of [Isaac] Watts and [Charles] Wesley alone, and he will become a fine theologian."[28] He undoubtedly had in mind hymns like "And Can it Be That I Should Gain" and "When I Survey the Wondrous Cross."

This was more than just advice. Tozer collected hymnals and was often seen on his way to an appointment with his face buried in one. He would spend hours on his knees with his Bible and his hymnal. In fact, he spent so much time in this position that he began wearing pants with reinforced material at the knees so that he wouldn't wear holes in them.

Tozer offered this profound advice:

Sometimes our hearts are strangely stubborn and will not soften or grow tender no matter how much praying we do. It is often found that the reading or singing of a good hymn will melt the ice jam and start the inward affections flowing once again. I say it without qualification; after the sacred scriptures, the next best companion for the soul is sacred music.[29]

Exalted Vision of Christ

One final legacy and, without doubt, the most critical contribution of A. W. Tozer is his exalted view of Christ. He had an ability to write in such a way that the reader's vision of God is transformed and taken to new heights.

In the opening line in his classic book on the attributes of God, Tozer declared, "What comes into our minds when we think about God is the most important thing about us."[30] I am so grateful Tozer was willing to put in the effort to elevate our thoughts about God.

On one occasion Tozer spent all night awake as the train he was on traveled from Chicago to Texas. He had asked the porter for a small table in his room, and there in his little compartment he began writing away.

Eventually, the porter became worried that the light was on and Tozer hadn't come to supper. He knocked on his door and asked, "Friend, would you like me to bring you something to eat?" Tozer never looked up but just mumbled, "Yes, bring me some toast and tea."

At the end of the train trip, Tozer walked into the station with a rough draft under his arm entitled *The Pursuit of God*. It sold more than a million copies. More importantly, it revealed the nature of God, when this teaching was being lost in his generation.

Tozer put the great doctrine of God's omniscience as simply as possible, writing, "[God] is never surprised, never amazed. He never wonders about anything nor (except when drawing men out for their own good) does He seek information or ask questions."[31]

James Boice explains why this truth that A. W. Tozer heralded is so critical to biblical Christianity:

> *God has never learned from anyone. God cannot learn. Could God at any time or in any manner receive into His mind knowledge that He did not possess and had not possessed from eternity, He would be less than Himself. To think of a God who must sit at the feet of a teacher, even*

though that teacher be an archangel, is to think of someone other than the Most High God, maker of heaven and earth. God knows effortlessly all matters, all relations, all causes, all thoughts, all mysteries, all feelings, all desires, every unuttered secret. God never discovers anything![32]

An Honest Appraisal

Now I could put a period here, and we might all wonder at how amazing A. W. Tozer was—a man who obviously lived on the mountaintops of intimacy with God. Yet the more you learn about someone, even someone like Tozer, the more you discover what ought to be emulated and what ought to be forgotten.

Even the apostle Paul wrote, "Be imitators of me, just as I also am of Christ" (1 Corinthians 11:1). In other words, "Don't just follow me for the sake of imitating me; imitate me insofar as you see me following after and imitating Jesus Christ." No Christian from the past or present should be considered or portrayed as perfect, with all the warts and bumps airbrushed away and the halo always sitting straight and shiny above the head.

The truth is, Tozer would never want accolades or tributes. He was well aware of many of his shortcomings and yet seemingly unaware of others.

One author said that Tozer battled depression. I wonder if it was something more akin to struggling with a deep sense of introspection. He often seemed muddled in a painfully silent fog.[33] It wasn't unusual for him to come to the family dinner table and not say a word, with everyone else at the table awkwardly afraid to do so.

After church services, Tozer often attempted to avoid people, shunning conversations and even slipping into the church nursery room until everyone had left. While he commended his wife's gift of hospitality, he disliked having people over to their home and even refused to allow his wife's family to visit their home, a decision that brought a great deal of hurt and frustration to his wife and their extended family.[34]

All but one of Tozer's six children, his youngest daughter, never felt close to him and grew estranged from him over the years.

Even though Tozer brought in thousands of dollars from book sales, he never explained why he refused to make his family's life—and the demands on his wife—more bearable by purchasing a family car. Instead, they were all, including Tozer, forced to use buses and trains and to borrow rides from other people. He always made sure they lived near enough to the church so they could all walk there.

We can only imagine how terribly difficult their home life was and the extra difficulties his wife had to endure because of his demanding frugality.

Three years after accepting a church in Canada, on the agreement that all he would have to do was preach, he suddenly died of a heart attack. He was sixty-six years old.

It was only after Tozer's death that his wife discovered that he had refused to purchase a pension. She also learned that he had given half his paychecks back to the churches he pastored and had taken no royalties from the millions of his books that had been sold.

Tozer is proof that it is possible to see God in fresh and intimate ways and still miss seeing other people around us—even those in our own family. The old adage that the cobbler's wife has no shoes is too often true. In some ways it was true even in the life of someone like A. W. Tozer.

He was a man whose mind and affections were so set on Christ above that he missed some things that needed attention on earth below. Certainly, we must guard against doing the same, even as we acknowledge that his advice and perspective still rings true—we are to seek the things above.

However, I fear that for the average Christian, the opposite is true. So much of our affection and attention is based on the things of earth that the things of Christ are never pursued with passion and singularity.

Not many of us will err on the side of Tozer. Would we give thousands of dollars away and force ourselves to ride a bus with our kids in tow?

Don't misunderstand. I think he should have bought a car. But, as Warren Wiersbe wrote of him, Tozer was in so many ways a man who walked to the beat of a different drummer.[35] He simply wanted God more than anything else. And he was never content with where he was in his pursuit of the glory of God.

Listen to a prayer he composed:

O God, I have tasted Thy goodness, and it has both satisfied me and made me thirsty for more. I am painfully conscious of my need of further grace. I am ashamed of my lack of desire. O God, the Triune God, I want to want Thee; I long to be filled with longing; I thirst to be more thirsty still. Show me Thy glory, I pray Thee, that so I may know Thee indeed. Begin in mercy a new work of love within me.... Give me grace to rise and follow Thee up from this misty lowland where I have wandered so long. In Jesus' name. Amen.[36]

SUSANNA WESLEY

While King Solomon walked with God during his early and middle-aged years, he earned a reputation for great wisdom. One of the most remarkable, yet unseen, credits to Solomon's life, was the testimony of the woman who became his early mentor and teacher.

The classic thirty-first chapter of the book of Proverbs opens with these words: "The words of King Lemuel, the oracle which his mother taught him." I believe Lemuel is one of several names in the Bible applied to Solomon.

We're told in 2 Samuel 12:24 that David named his son Solomon. The next verse tells us that God also gave Solomon a name: "Now the Lord loved him and sent word through Nathan the prophet, and he named him Jedidiah for the Lord's sake." Jedidiah simply means "loved by the Lord."

If two names aren't enough of a legacy, there was a third name: Lemuel. I agree with those Old Testament scholars who see this, not as a proper name, but as a term of dedication, evidently given to Solomon personally by his own mother. Lemuel means, "For God."

Solomon's mother, you may recall, was Bathsheba. Solomon was the second son born to her and King David. The first son died in infancy. Bathsheba evidently dedicated Solomon back to God. Solomon used that special name she gave him, Lemuel, in Proverbs 31 as he presented those classic principles of a godly woman his mother gave him.

One of the striking things about the book of Proverbs is how often Solomon's proverbs challenge us to listen, not only to the advice of our fathers, which we would expect, but also to the counsel of our mothers.

For instance, Solomon writes, "Hear, my son, your father's instruction and do not forsake your mother's teaching; indeed, they are a graceful wreath to your head and ornaments about your neck" (Proverbs 1:8-9). In other words, he's saying, "Listen up when your father gives you godly advice, and don't take your mother's counsel any less lightly. Listen to her as well!"

If you dig back into church history some three hundred years or so, you'll find one particular woman who stands out as a wonderful example of one who attempted to live up to the responsibility to teach and counsel her children with biblical truth. Her name was Susanna Wesley. She was born into a pastor's family in 1669.

To set the stage, the seventeenth and early eighteenth centuries were among the worst years in England's history. One author wrote that England had degenerated into a moral cesspool, and the evidence she cites certainly backs such an assessment.

Thomas Carlyle, the nineteenth-century philosopher and author, said that England had a stomach that was well alive, but the soul was dead. William Blackstone visited the church of every major clergyman in London during this same period and later wrote that in most sermons it was impossible to tell whether the preacher was a follower of Mohammed or Christ. Gambling was so extensive that one historian called England a vast casino. Newborns were left exposed to die in the streets just as in late Roman days. Tickets to public executions were sold as if people were attending the theatre.

The same author wrote, "Historians now recognize that the nation of England changed course in the 18th century largely through the Great Awakening and the ministry of George Whitfield and John Wesley and others [including John Wesley's brother, Charles]."[37]

Most people know of the early leaders of Methodism, John and Charles Wesley. Rather few know much about the woman who served as their early teacher and mentor, their mother Susanna.

Susanna was born into the home of a London pastor and his wife. She was the youngest of twenty-five children. You read that right—twenty-five children! As you might expect, the family suffered through poverty.

Susanna's father passed down to his youngest daughter his own passionate personality for justice and the holiness of God. He gave her a backbone of steel. An invitation he received to preach to Parliament reveals the kind of man Susanna's father was. As his text for that occasion, he chose Job 27:5, which reads, "Far be it from me that I should declare you right," or as the King James puts it, "God forbid that I should justify you." He was never invited back.

Marriage and Challenges

During her father's ministry, which grew tremendously, young seminarians would often visit in their home. On one occasion a young man named Samuel Wesley came for a visit. Susanna was thirteen at the time, and Samuel was nineteen. They struck up a friendship, and a few years later they married. Their first child was born a year after that.

Although Samuel was an Oxford-educated scholar, he was placed by the Church of England in a small country parish, 150 miles from London. The couple's parsonage was literally a mud hut with no glass in the windows, just wooden shutters.

One of the forgotten aspects of ministry during these terrible days of spiritual darkness was the price paid by those who preached the gospel. In my research, I cataloged the following abuses delivered by people living around the Wesleys—some even from people who attended the church:

* They demonstrated their displeasure by mocking the children.

* They burned the family crops.

* They damaged the parsonage, burning it to the ground on one occasion.

* They slit the udder of the family cow so she couldn't give milk.

* They even killed the family dog.

On one occasion a group of villagers upset over Samuel's political views gathered around the parsonage, not knowing that Samuel was away on church business and Susanna and her children were there alone. They shouted through the entire night, beating on drums, and firing their guns.

Susanna was just recovering from delivering her sixteenth child. The baby's nurse was so exhausted after the night of commotion that she lapsed into a deep sleep, rolling over on the baby and smothering it.

A few years later, in 1709, the Wesleys' home caught fire in the middle of the night, allegedly torched by villagers. The family members all scrambled outside to safety, including Susanna, who was expecting a child at the time. When they got outside, they did a head count and discovered they were missing one of their children, six-year-old John.

He had awakened later than the rest and was unable to go down the stairs because of the fire. He stood on a chest by the open window and was spotted from down below. One neighbor lifted another neighbor up on his shoulders so the second man could snatch John to safety just moments before the roof fell in. "John saw his deliverance as God's work and for many years referred to himself as a literal 'brand snatched from the burning.'"[38]

Their troubles didn't end there. On another occasion a parishioner demanded immediate payment of a debt. Unable to pay the debt, Samuel was put into debtor's prison.

After a while you might ask God to call you into something a little safer. We have little idea today of what it meant back then to preach the truth as it relates to current issues of the day.

John Wesley would later have his own pulpit in London designed so that it could be entered only from the balcony and could not be accessed from the congregation below. It was designed that way to protect him.

Once, John preached against the evil of slavery, and members of the congregation rioted, breaking apart the pews. John escaped up and through the balcony to his office. I've stood in his pulpit in England and marveled at his courage. He was well prepared by watching his own parents suffer greatly.

Mother and Teacher

None of Susanna and Samuel's ministry challenges would compare to the pain of losing so many of their children. In their first seven years of marriage, Susanna would deliver seven children; three would die. In fact, she would end up delivering nineteen children. But only ten of them would survive childhood.

To those surviving children Susanna literally dedicated her life. She committed herself to living out the book of Proverbs, teaching and counseling the minds and hearts of her children.

Susanna refused to teach her children formally until they turned five. Then their education began in earnest. She expected them to memorize the entire alphabet on their first day of school.[39]

The Wesley daughters were not excluded either. In this regard, Susanna was undoubtedly influenced by the fact that her father had taught her to read and allowed her to roam in his vast library when she was a little girl.

So, the girls, along with the boys, learned Latin, Greek, Hebrew, poetry, the classics, history, and music. Susanna would teach them three hours in the morning and three hours in the afternoon.

All were on a schedule from the moment they awoke at 6:00 a.m. till the day wound down with an hour of personal study in Scripture by each child before candles were snuffed out at exactly 8:00 p.m. As one writer said, Susanna was "the queen of structure."[40]

She would tell others that she didn't want her children to become educated ruffians and so they were taught manners and obedience. They were to remain silent at the dinner table, play only with selected companions, required to speak in precise English.[41] As has often been noted, Susanna clearly believed that for children to grow into self-disciplined adults, they must first be parent-disciplined children.

If you've read Susanna Wesley's biography, you know she became rather famous for her rules of conduct. I have come across several different versions of those rules, but they all say the same basic thing. Some of her rules are as follows:

* No sinful act should pass without punishment.
* No child should be punished twice for the same fault.
* Promises are to be strictly enforced and observed.
* Teach them to fear the rod.
* Eating between meals is not allowed.
* They are to be taught to pray as soon as they can speak.
* Give them nothing they cry for, but only what they ask for politely.
* Any intention toward obedience, even if the performance was not as well as it should have been, is to be accepted and encouraged.

But she wasn't interested only in order and academics and good manners. She wanted her children to reverence the Lord above all, to live holy lives.

In a letter, she told her son John that a child is capable of being governed by righteous thinking only "when the will of a child is totally subdued, and it is brought to revere and stand in awe of the parents."[42]

One writer described the Wesley children as "a cluster of bright, . . . argumentative boys and girls, living by a clean and high code, and on the plainest fare . . . with learning as an ideal, duty as an atmosphere and fear of God as law."[43]

Sometimes Susanna took matters into her own hands—even if it went against cultural norms and raised some eyebrows.

Once, her husband appointed another man, a Mr. Inman, to preach the Sunday sermons while he was in London for an extended period defending another minister against charges of heresy. Evidently, the man wasn't up to the job, and the sermons were boring, stale meanderings.

Susanna promptly began an afternoon service for the family, gathering them to sing a few psalms and pray. She then read a sermon selected from a book in her husband's library. While the service originally was meant only for the Wesley household, others found out about it and began attending. Before long, the parsonage, and the lawn was overflowing with more than two hundred people, while the Sunday morning service dwindled to nothing.

Mr. Inman wrote to Samuel and complained that his wife had begun a competing worship service. Samuel wrote to his wife telling her to stop immediately. She replied to her husband that the meetings were having a genuine and effective ministry to those who attended and that Mr. Inman was the only one objecting.

The services continued.[44]

We can imagine with all the activity and challenges of this household that Susanna never had any time alone. She struggled to find a secret place to get away, and so she finally gave up, telling her children that when they saw her with her apron over her head, she was in prayer and could not be disturbed. Imagine, the only way to get alone was to hide out under an apron, pulled over your head!

Still, she found time, not only for herself and her children, but also for each child individually. When she was teaching eight of her children, she had a plan to spend one hour a week talking with each child.

> On Monday it was Mollie.
> On Tuesday it was Hetty.
> Wednesday was for Nancy.
> Thursday held an hour for Jacky (John).
> Friday was Patty's day.
> Saturday was little Charles's day.
> And Sunday, two hours were devoted to Emelia and Sukey (Susanna).[45]

She was dedicated to providing the counsel of a mother to her children.

A Realistic Perspective

Like other people we study in this series, it's tempting to put a period right about here and leave well enough alone. In fact, most of what I knew previously about Susanna and Samuel Wesley ended here.

But other factors are worth noting. Indeed, in order to benefit from the godly examples we study, we must have a realistic perspective of them as it relates to the home, raising children, educating children, marriage, and ministry. And this means certain realities must not be hidden behind closed doors.

When we make people out to be nearly perfect examples of godliness, we not only create heroes out of clay pots, but we also assume that if we do everything they did, our lives will be as satisfied and fulfilled as their lives. We think that if we use all Susanna Wesley's sixteen rules of conduct, make sure our kids' lives are structured and they're in bed by 8:00 p.m., and have devotions under an apron, maybe we'll have the kind of home Samuel and Susanna had. Maybe our children will all become active participants, even leaders, in another great awakening.

The truth is, Samuel and Susanna struggled their entire marriage with inflexible personalities and stubborn wills.

Samuel once prayed at the dinner table for the king, and at the end everyone said "amen" except Susanna. He demanded to know why, and she simply told him that King William of Orange was not the rightful king but that King James II was the one who should be on the throne. Samuel stood to his feet, in front of the children and demanded she repent and say "amen." She refused. He then said, "Well, we must part ways, for if there are two kings, then we shall have two beds." And he left the house in a fury.

A couple months later, he returned to see if she'd changed her mind, and she hadn't, after which he told her he would leave and never see her or the children again. It wasn't the first time he'd left in a rage, and it wouldn't be the last.

On his way out of town, Samuel met another clergyman, who persuaded him to persist in his marriage vows regardless of his wife's political views. Samuel relented and upon his return to the house, he discovered the parsonage was on fire, more than likely set afire by villagers.

Samuel stayed and rebuilt the parsonage, reconciling with Susanna. Their fifteenth child, John Wesley, was born a year later.

Other issues plagued their marriage and their home life. Samuel was not only a poor money manager, but evidently he didn't try too hard to repay his debts as he should. He went to jail twice for failing to pay his bills.

He reached beyond his own abilities in several failed attempts to make money. For instance, he was convinced that what the church really needed was an exhaustive commentary on the Book of Job—written in Latin, which the average person couldn't read.

Samuel used most of the family's meager funds to finance this publication, which then never sold. He then tried publishing poetry, but it was an embarrassment and became a joke in the community.

He seemed oblivious to it all. Perhaps you've seen that lack of self-objectivity in certain people who are convinced they are good at something, but no one is willing to tell them the truth.

As a result, the Wesleys lived on the edge of destitution and were perpetually in debt due to Samuel's stubbornness. In fact, his debts were never fully repaid until after he died. Whatever consistency there was in the home was due primarily to Susanna's efforts.

While the world knows about two of her children, the truth is, Susanna was challenged and heartbroken over and over again with children who chose not to walk with Christ despite all her efforts.

Susanna and Samuel's daughter Susanna, nicknamed Sukey, chose to marry an unbeliever who ended up physically abusing her. She nearly died in childbirth and, suffering from her husband's cruelty, finally fled with her children to London, never reconciling with her husband.

Another daughter, Emilia, also fell in love with an unbeliever but ended the relationship after her brothers counseled her. This is further evidence that a relationship with her father was virtually nonexistent. Unfortunately, at the age of forty-four, Emilia was so concerned that she might never marry that she married too quickly a man without proof of genuine character. He soon took her life savings and left her with his debts and their dying baby.

Another daughter, Hetty, ran off with a lawyer who promised her a future home and marriage. A few months later, he changed his mind, and she returned home, disgraced and pregnant. Sadly, Samuel disowned her and then foolishly demanded that she marry a local plumber to rescue her reputation. She agreed, but the two endured an unhappy marriage.

Finally, their daughter Martha also married a man without genuine spiritual interests. He was often unfaithful to her, bringing home illegitimate children whom she raised as if they were her own. Her husband eventually left with another woman and died overseas.[46]

Samuel's repeated abandonment of the family, his unwillingness to manage his household well, and his stubborn arrogance that demanded applause for his minor achievements while overlooking the needs of his wife and daughters left them without a shepherd and counselor. This brought great difficulty and pain into Susanna's life.

Susanna once wrote a prayer while in the crucible of pain that sheds light on her commitment to the sovereign purposes of God. She prayed, "All my sufferings, by the admirable management of Omnipotent Goodness, have concurred to promote my spiritual and eternal good ... glory be to Thee, O Lord."[47]

While several of her children strayed from the faith she so

persistently taught them, two of her children, especially, embraced the faith and ultimately had a profound impact upon the world for Christ—John and Charles Wesley. As a result, Susanna Wesley, who neither preached a sermon nor published a book, became known as the Mother of Methodism.

Her son Charles wrote more than six thousand hymns, and John preached to at least a million people as the Methodist movement took England by storm. The movement took its name from the methodical, systematic patterns of life they adopted, which ironically mirrored the brothers' structured upbringing under the tutelage and counsel of their mother.

Unlike her husband, Susanna said late in life, "I am content to fill a little space if God be glorified."[48]

When his father Samuel died, John Wesley moved his mother into his ministry headquarters, which included a church, a school, a clinic, and living quarters. A host of people lived at the headquarters as the movement grew, and Susanna served the people involved with great humility and joy.

Susanna passed away on July 23, 1742. Most of her children had gathered in these final days. Her last command to her children was simply this: "Children, as soon as I am released, sing a song of praise to God."[49]

Her son John bought land near her burial site and built a home there. He positioned his desk near a window facing the cemetery where she was buried.

It was a way of being reminded of the importance of heeding his mother's example and advice and the message of Solomon, which is repeated in Proverbs 6:20-21 and paraphrased as follows:

> *Follow your father's good advice; don't wander off from your mother's teachings. Wrap yourself in them from*

head to foot; wear them like a scarf around your neck. Wherever you walk, they'll guide you; whenever you rest, they'll guard you; when you wake up, they'll tell you what's next. For sound advice is a beacon, good teaching is a light, moral discipline is a life path. (MSG)

OSWALD CHAMBERS

In 1890, a fifteen-year-old boy and his father were walking home from a meeting where they had just heard Charles Spurgeon preach. The young man said to his father that he would have gladly given himself to the Lord had the opportunity been given. The boy's father responded, "You can do it now, my boy." They stopped there on the path and prayed together.

That young man was Oswald Chambers. He would later join a Baptist church in London and eventually enter art school, determined to be an artist, a poet, and a musician for life.

Three years later he felt he should study for the ministry, and so he abandoned his art studies and enrolled at the Dunoon Training College in Scotland. He did so well academically that he was invited to remain as a tutor following his graduation.

However, it was during this period of time that he entered into what he would later call "the dark night of his soul," a time of doubt and discouragement over his lackluster spirituality—a disconnect from what we would call a personal relationship with Christ. He tried in vain to arrive at some sort of sanctified state of self-satisfaction, a state his Pentecostal friends referred to as the mountaintop of victory.

Chambers wrote a poem about that period in his life that included these lyrics:

> O Lord Jesus, hear my crying
> For a consecrated life.
> For I bite the dust in trying
> For release from this dark strife.[50]

That dark period ended with a personal commitment and

surrender to God's Spirit, something Oswald referred to as a baptism of the Holy Spirit.

Oswald was simply borrowing the vocabulary of his association with the Holiness and Pentecostal Movements. While he didn't speak in tongues—in fact, he decried any attempt to prove that the baptism of the Holy Spirit was the same thing as speaking in tongues—he was no doubt influenced in his early days by these movements. For a brief period of time, he represented the Prayer League, a ministry funded by the early Holiness Movement in England.

Writing of Oswald's experience and analyzing what happened to him in more biblical terminology, Warren Wiersbe implies that Oswald may simply have been genuinely converted at this time.[51]

Oswald eventually enrolled at the University of Edinburgh to prepare for ministry. While there, he was deeply influenced by the preaching and ministry of Alexander Whyte, a preacher cut from the same mold as Charles Spurgeon.

So, Oswald Chambers was influenced early on by the gospel preaching of Charles Spurgeon; alerted to the need for total surrender to the Holy Spirit by Pentecostal friends; and tutored from the pulpit by Alexander Whyte. And that wasn't all. He would later be influenced by D. L. Moody's life and ministry through an organization Oswald would join as a chaplain, essentially becoming a foreign missionary serving with the YMCA.

Most people have no idea that the YMCA used to send out missionaries. However, the YMCA Paris Resolution, written in 1855, shows the movement was organized around a twofold purpose: "To unite young men who, regarding Jesus Christ as their God and Savior according to the Holy Scripture, desire to be His disciples in their doctrine and in their life, and [second] to associate their efforts for the extension of His Kingdom among young men."[52]

Before joining the YMCA, Oswald toured the world, preaching as an itinerate evangelist. His tour took him primarily to America and Japan for some ten years.

When he was in his early thirties, on one particular passage to America, he was asked by Christian friends to keep an eye on a young woman her friends called "Biddy." She was traveling alone to America in search of work.

He was happy to oblige her concerned friends, and he kept an eye on her. In fact, he married her twenty-four months later so that he could permanently keep an eye on her.

Their union, in 1910 would ultimately create a ministry of which neither one of them could have possibly dreamed. Biddy was a trained and skillful stenographer who could take shorthand at the rate of 250 words a minute. She began recording everything Oswald taught and preached.

A few years later, Chambers became convinced that a Bible college was needed in England that would emphasize both a personal relationship with Christ and academic excellence. The school began and operated on the principle of faith. In fact, the Bible college was never more than a month away from having to close for lack of funds.

Yet Oswald was so committed to praying and receiving whatever the Lord wanted to provide that when a wealthy friend once offered to completely endow the Bible college, Oswald responded, "No thank you, because, if you do that, the school might go on longer than God wants."[53]

It's little wonder that Oswald Chambers failed to fit in perfectly with the religious conventions of his day. In fact, he was nicknamed, the Apostle of the Haphazard. His ministry path seemed erratic to many; his life plan wasn't ironed out and smooth. He went from one adventure of faith to another without so much as a worry.

When World War I broke out, he struggled to remain at his Bible college in England. He wanted to serve on the fields, close to the action. However, he was not so impetuous that he would not yield to the Holy Spirit. He prayed,

> Lord, I praise You for this place I am in, but the wonder has begun to stir in me—is this Your place for me? Hold me steady doing Your will. It may be only restlessness; if so, calm me to strength that I sin not against You by doubting.[54]

A year later Oswald Chambers became convinced God wanted him overseas. He suspended the Bible college indefinitely and left for Egypt, with Biddy and their little girl following two months later. He set up camp as a YMCA chaplain to the troops stationed at a military base just outside Cairo, Egypt.

Chambers found the whole situation intriguing. Cairo assaulted his physical senses with enticing aromas from street-side cafés and the eerie Muslim calls to prayer from countless minarets. Spiritually, the challenge of taking the gospel to several thousand men in a busy military camp seemed almost staggering.[55] But here he came.

When he arrived to join the other missionaries, he immediately instituted changes. Among other changes, he informed his fellow YMCA workers that they would immediately abandon weekly movies and concerts for Bible classes. He was going to begin teaching the soldiers the Bible.

The other workers predicted the soldiers would leave in a mass exodus from the wooden YMCA building—or hut, as it was called—built in the military camp. But instead of a mass exodus, there was an awakening. It wasn't long before several hundred soldiers packed into the YMCA hut to listen to his thought-provoking, humor-punctuated biblical messages.

He also began a weekly prayer meeting that was predicted to fail as well. It began with two other men but soon grew to fill the hut. Because so many of these men knew they might never return home alive, the gospel became the water of living hope; prayer became their only source of strength.

A Signature Verse

It wasn't long before Oswald Chambers's key verse became known to the entire camp. He had a banner created with the words of Luke 11:13 stretching the width of the platform: "How much more will your heavenly Father give the Holy Spirit to those who ask Him?"

Everyone was confronted with that text throughout Oswald Chambers's ministry. Let's look briefly at his signature ministry verse.

In the carnage of World War I, we can imagine how much these soldiers wanted to know if God heard their prayers and cared and what kind of prayer makes it through to God. The disciples seemed to have the same questions. In Luke 11:1, we read, "It happened that while Jesus was praying in a certain place, after He had finished, one of His disciples said to Him, "Lord, teach us to pray."

Interestingly, the disciples never asked Jesus to teach them how to walk on water, silence a storm, or feed thousands of people with a handful of bread and fish. Rather, they requested that He teach them to pray. The Lord responded over the next few verses by giving us the Disciples' Prayer—although the church calls it the Lord's Prayer.

Following this instruction, the Lord anticipated the next question on the hearts of the disciples: Does God the Father really answer prayer? Jesus created one of His amazing stories to address this issue and to prove an important point. Notice verses 5-6:

Then He said to them, "Suppose one of you has a friend, and goes to him at midnight and says to him, "Friend, lend me three loaves [three pieces of flat bread]; for a friend of mine has come to me from a journey, and I have nothing to set before him."

Don't miss the fact that you're going over to your friend's house at *midnight*. That's not exactly the most convenient time to knock on your neighbor's door.

However, in that culture, traveling at night wasn't unusual during hot weather. So, without warning, you just might have a visitor arriving at midnight. Also, hospitality was considered a social duty, particularly in Israel. So now you've got a dilemma on your hands. It's late at night, and you don't have anything to feed your guest!

I remember learning something about hospitality as I was growing up in a missionary home. It seemed like someone was always visiting in our home. Many nights I gave up my bedroom for a traveling missionary or preacher or guest. My mother always seemed to have meals ready; food just seemed to miraculously appear. I had no idea that she kept meals waiting in the freezer for that next surprise guest.

Marsha and I had been married for only a couple of months, and I was just beginning my seminary training. One Sunday night, a missionary couple I knew from my past showed up at our church. After the service, I asked them where they were eating supper, and they said they didn't have any plans. So I said, "Why don't you come over to our apartment for dinner?"

They were thrilled, and they followed us home in their car. On the way, Marsha was looking straight ahead, but she was talking to me. She was saying, "Honey, we don't have anything to eat. The cupboard is bare, and I planned to go get some groceries after work tomorrow. We don't have any food for dinner."

That wasn't all she said, but that's all you need to know. She was sweet about it, though.

Then suddenly she said, "Wait, I've got a head of lettuce and some cheese." When we got home, she whipped up a Caesar salad fit for royalty.

After dinner I made the mistake of asking this couple, "So where are you staying tonight?" They said, "We don't have any plans."

Marsha actually insisted they sleep in our only bedroom, and she and I made a pallet on the floor in the living room. I was going to be sleeping out there anyway, so this was an improvement.

The lesson I learned was this: Don't invite anybody over for dinner without checking with your wife to see if you have anything to eat.

In Jesus' story you're stuck with an overnight guest, and you don't have a choice! Ah, but your neighbors were baking bread earlier in the afternoon, and you know your only hope is to ask them for some of it.

But here's the dilemma: you can either be a bad host and send your guest to bed hungry, or you can be a bad neighbor by going next door and waking up the sleeping family.[56]

Now look at verse 7: "And from inside he [your neighbor] answers and says, 'Do not bother me; the door has already been shut and my children and I are in bed.'"

Bed in that day was a mat on the floor where the entire family usually slept. Furthermore, in the villages of Christ's day, it was customary to bring the chickens and goats into their homes at night so they wouldn't be stolen.

Getting up at midnight would awaken the entire family and a bunch of animals along with them. No wonder the neighbor says to go away and stop bothering him.

But Jesus says in verse 8 that the neighbor will finally get up and give you bread, not because he's your friend, but because you're going to wake everybody up anyway if he doesn't help you.

Now unfortunately, many Christians think this story proves that you have to keep knocking on heaven's door until you finally convince God to answer you. That is, God only answers the prayers of the persistent.

Now obviously there is something to be said about persistence in prayer. We are to pray without ceasing (1 Thessalonians 5:17). But that is not at all the point Jesus is making here.

The point of this story is not one of *comparison* between God and this sleepy, irritated neighbor; rather, it's a story of *contrast*.

God isn't like this sleepy neighbor at all. We can come to Him anytime, and His door is open. This is what Jesus goes on to say in Luke 11:9: "So I say to you, ask and it will be given to you; seek, and you will find; knock, and it will be opened to you." We simply come to Him and ask. God's door will be opened to us—guaranteed.

Look at the way Jesus reinforces this idea in verses 11-12: "Now suppose one of you fathers is asked by his son for a fish; he will not give him a snake instead of a fish, will he? Of if he is asked for an egg, he will not give him a scorpion, will he?" The answer to these questions is obvious: of course not!

Jesus then concludes, "If you then, being evil, know how to give good gifts to your children, how much more will your heavenly Father give the Holy Spirit to those who ask Him?" (Luke 11:13).

Here's the point: If earthly, flesh-and-blood fathers, who are fallen, sinful creatures, give good gifts to their children, imagine how our immortal, sinless Father treats His children! Indeed, He gives us communion with the Holy Spirit, including power for service and spiritual fruitfulness—the best gifts of all—to those who ask Him.

This doesn't absolve us from intensity and discipline in prayer, but it does mean we do not have to wring from God the Father's unwilling hands the things we really need. In fact, our heavenly Father already knows what we need, and our greatest need is Himself.[57]

His answers to our prayers may not always be what we want or expect, but whatever arrives, comes from the open, giving, and gracious hand of our sovereign God who gives us the Holy Spirit so that we can handle and joyously receive whatever answer He gives us.

I like the way one author summarized this lesson from Jesus:

You ask for a gift, and God the Father gives you the Giver.
You ask for a product, and He gives you the source.
You ask for comfort, and He gives you the Comforter.
You come seeking power, and He gives you the source of power.
You need help, and He gives you the Helper.
You seek answers, and He gives you the indwelling Spirit of truth.[58]

Prayer is a large part of our walk of faith. We come to the Lord in faith, believing the promises He has given and anticipating His good answers, even when we do not understand them all. Oswald Chambers said, "Faith is deliberate confidence in the character of God whose ways you may not understand at the time." He also said, "Faith never knows where it is being led, but it loves and knows the One who is leading. . . . The life of faith is not a life of mounting up with wings but a life of walking and not fainting."[59]

Death and Lasting Impact

Unlike his spiritual mentors Charles Spurgeon, D. L. Moody, and Alexander Whyte, Oswald Chambers would remain obscure, virtually unheard of, during his lifetime. In fact, he once said to a friend, "I feel I shall be buried for a time, hidden away in obscurity; then suddenly I shall flame out, do my work, and be gone."[60]

In a way that is exactly what happened. After less than twenty-four months of ministry in Egypt, Chambers developed appendicitis. He resisted going to a hospital on the grounds that the beds were needed by men wounded in battle.

Eventually, as his condition became critical, on October 29, a surgeon performed an emergency appendectomy. For a few weeks his life hung in the balance. Then he seemed to revive, only to suffer from hemorrhaging in his lungs. On November 15, 1917, just two years after arriving in Egypt for ministry that seemed so amazingly blessed by God's Spirit, and to the utter shock of his wife, family, supporting friends, and the men he served, Oswald Chambers died. He was only forty-three years of age.

Though he was teaching a hut full of soldiers at an obscure missionary outpost near Cairo, Egypt, when he died, Oswald Chambers's life and ministry would eventually impact millions of Christians over the next several generations. And his influence is still felt today due to the diligent work of his wife.

After Oswald's death, Biddy eventually returned home with the couple's daughter. Sensing the Lord's will in the matter, Biddy took out all her notes from her husband's sermons and lessons, notes she had taken in shorthand as he had preached and taught at the Bible college, in Japan, in America, and in Egypt.

Through what she recorded, edited, and published, the

world heard from Oswald Chambers. To this day, his messages continue to provide wise, personal, challenging, homespun biblical wisdom on many subjects.

Important Themes

Of the many subjects Chambers addressed, I want to comment on just a few important themes found in his writings.

The Reading of Books

Like Spurgeon before him, Chambers encouraged his students to read widely. Spurgeon once said that a man who doesn't read will never be read, and a teacher who never quotes will never be quoted. Oswald Chambers was a voracious reader, and his lessons were sprinkled with the quotes of others.

He said, "When people refer to 'a man as a man of one book,' meaning the Bible, he is generally found to be a man of multitudinous books, which simply isolates the one Book to its proper grandeur."[61]

He also said, "Books are available counselors and preachers, always at hand . . . having this advantage over oral instructors, that they are ready to repeat their lesson as often as we please."[62]

Attention to Details

Chambers believed that every detail matters. He was always trying to improve the look of the huts and tents used by the YMCA. He was quoted as saying,

> A grave defect in much work of today is that we do not follow Solomon's admonition, 'Whatsoever thy hand findeth to do, do it with thy might.' The tendency, is to argue, 'It's only for so short a time, why trouble with it?' If it is only for five minutes, let it be well done.[63]

You might think that with this kind of attitude, he would be someone you wanted to avoid. But that was hardly the case.

Humor and a Joyful Spirit

Chambers loved to laugh. And he did something fairly novel in that he expected his audience to laugh at times as well—and he would laugh along. He wrote in his journal, "Lord, keep me radiantly and joyously Thine."[64]

One man complained to his wife about Oswald's incessant humor. He wrote a letter to Mrs. Chambers in which he said, "Your husband is the most irreverent Reverend I've ever met!"[65]

Indeed, what kind of missionary tells his audience, as Chambers did, "Keep praying and playing and being yourself."[66] That's not exactly a typical message.

Often his humor disarmed people and drove home his point. He said once, "Have we ever got into the way of letting God work, or are we so amazingly important that we really wonder . . . what the Almighty does before we get up in the morning!"[67]

Oswald gave his students this wonderful advice: "Never make a principle out of your own experience; let God be as original with other people as He is with you."[68] Oswald Chambers was definitely an original.

Decision Making

Oswald Chambers's counsel regarding decision making was simply this: Trust God and do the next thing. In other words, make sure you're walking with God; and if you are, don't hesitate to do whatever the next thing on your plate happens to be.

And with that counsel, Chambers took away so much of the mystery of God's will. Trust God; then, with confidence and joy, do the next thing you want to do.

This principle of decision making is based in faith in God and a proper fear of God. Chambers said, "The remarkable thing about fearing God is that when you fear God you fear nothing else, whereas if you do not fear God you fear everything else."[69]

I found it interesting that Oswald once said that the only lasting preaching is preaching with a pen. Yet he never wrote one book.

Even though there are some thirty books with his name as the author, including his famous devotional entitled *My Utmost for His Highest*, they were all pieced together by Biddy Chambers. Millions of copies of *My Utmost for His Highest* have been sold, and it's been translated into thirty-nine languages—and counting.

When Biddy Chambers died in 1966, she was involved in the latest edition of *My Utmost for His Highest*. After Biddy's death, their daughter took up the work and was involved in even more writing projects using her father's material until she too passed away in 1997.

They followed the advice of Oswald Chambers: pray for God's wisdom through His Spirit, trust Him, and then do the next thing, whatever it might be that God wants you to do.

ADONIRAM JUDSON

In John 12, the Lord Jesus spoke to His disciples, foretelling His death, resurrection, and glorification. However, the Lord did not speak prophetically only of his own death but also of all those who, to this very day, surrender their lives to follow Christ no matter what.

He said, "Truly, truly, I say to you, unless a grain of wheat falls into the earth and dies, it remains alone; but if it dies, it bears much fruit" (John 12:24).

Jesus certainly implied that suffering and fruit-bearing go hand in hand. In fact, there seems to be a parallel between suffering much and having much influence for the glory of Christ.

Why is it that the people we study, both in the Bible and throughout church history, who accomplished so much for the Lord also suffered so much? In fact, it is often because they suffered that we study them. And, so, they are still influencing our world for Christ.

The words of our Lord as He entered Jerusalem, knowing that within days He would be crucified, still echo with this lasting principle: A legacy of spiritual fruit belongs to that man or woman who says to Christ, "Here am I; bury me. Here am I, willing even to die."

This description by our Lord of a fruitful life of surrender certainly fits the man who became America's first foreign missionary. He experienced incredible suffering. He buried several of his children; he dug graves for his first wife and then his second wife nineteen years later. Many of his associates died from disease and stress.

Long after becoming a living legend, this man of God wrote these words to potential missionary candidates:

It may be profitable to bear in mind, that a large proportion of those who come out on a mission to the East die within five years after leaving their native land. Walk softly, therefore; death is narrowly watching your steps. [70]

How's that for a recruiting strategy? Are you willing to be a seed, planted in the ground to suffer and even die to bear a harvest for the gospel of Jesus Christ?

Early Life and Unbelief

That missionary's name was Adoniram Judson. He was born into a pastor's home in 1788, in Malden, Massachusetts.

By the age of three, it was obvious he was a quick learner. To her surprise, his mother was able to teach him to read in just one week while his father was away preaching. Upon his father's return, Adoniram surprised him by reading an entire chapter from the Bible.[71]

When he was sixteen, his father enrolled him in Rhode Island College (now Brown University) because he considered Harvard and Yale too liberal. Adoniram excelled in his studies and graduated as valedictorian in 1807.

However, he held a secret that he didn't reveal until after his twentieth birthday. When he told his parents, their hearts were broken.[72]

Adoniram had been heavily influenced by a fellow student named Jacob Eames. Eames was popular, brilliant, artistic, and an unbeliever. He became one of Adoniram's closest friends and introduced him to what was called freethinking—really skepticism and atheism. By the time Adoniram graduated, he had abandoned the Bible he'd learned to read at the age of three and the gospel of his parents' faith.

After informing his parents of his unbelief and trying his hand at tutoring for a year, he set out to tour New England on horseback.

He eventually joined a group of actors in New York City, living what he called a "reckless, vagabond life." They would find lodging for a time and then slip out without paying their bills.[73] After only a few weeks, Adoniram grew tired of this undisciplined lifestyle and struck out on his own, roaming without purpose.

One evening he stopped to spend the night at an inn. The innkeeper warned him that his sleep might be interrupted by a man in the room next to Judson's room who was violently ill.

Sure enough, during the night, the moans and cries of the man in the next room kept him awake. The man seemed to be on the brink of death. Adoniram wondered about the man's soul. Where would he spend eternity? What was his hope after death? In fact, Adoniram would recount later how he himself lay there thinking the same thoughts about his own soul and his own life and his own eternal destiny.

Eventually the moaning stopped, and Adoniram drifted off to sleep. Early the next morning as he was leaving, Adoniram asked about the man, and the innkeeper told him the man had died during the night. Adoniram asked, "Do you know who he was?" The Innkeeper replied, "Oh yes. Young man from the college in Providence. Name was Eames, Jacob Eames."[74]

Adoniram could barely move. He pondered the death of his friend. "That hell should open in that country inn and snatch Jacob Eames, his dearest friend and guide, from the next room—this could not, simply could not, be pure coincidence."[75]

Conversion, Missions, and Marriage

It was clear to Adoniram Judson that God was on his trail. He immediately returned home to the joy of his parents. Months later he trusted Christ for his personal salvation and devoted himself entirely to the Lord.

Two years later, Adoniram finished seminary studies and applied for missionary status with the Congregational mission board. He had read a sermon as a student that had sparked his interest in the mission fields of India, Burma, and China, and he determined to give his life to serve Christ in that part of the world.

While his parents were thrilled with his conversion, they were not happy with his desire for missionary service overseas. He was offered a faculty position at Brown University, which he declined, much to their chagrin. He was offered a paid pastoral position nearby, which he declined, to his mother's tears.

On the same day he presented himself to the Congregational missionary board, he met a young woman named Ann Hasseltine. Over the next few weeks, they fell in love.

Adoniram was clear with his life's goal. He told Ann—and everyone else—that he was heading for Burma, located between southern India and China and now known as Myanmar. Ann was just as committed to the gospel and missionary work as he was.

One month after meeting Ann, he asked her father if he could marry her. His letter to Ann's father reveals his passion for the lost, but it also became prophetic of their future.

> *I have now to ask, whether you can consent to part with your daughter early next spring, to see her no more in this world; whether you can consent to her departure for a heathen land, and her subjection to the hardships and*

sufferings of a missionary life? whether you can consent to her exposure to the dangers of the ocean; to the fatal influence of the southern climate of India; to every kind of want and distress; to degradation, insult, persecution and perhaps a violent death? Can you consent to all this, for the sake of Him who left His heavenly home, and died for her and for you—for the sake of perishing immortal souls —for the sake of Zion, and the glory of God? Can you consent to all this, in hope of soon meeting your daughter in the world of glory with a crown of righteousness, brightened by the acclamations of praise which shall redound to her Saviour from heathens saved, through her means, from eternal woe and despair?[76]

How's that for a proposal? I'd like to take your daughter away from you to a pagan land, where she'll probably suffer every deprivation until she eventually dies, most likely, violently.

Ann wrote to a friend, "I have . . . come to the determination to give up all my comforts and enjoyments here, sacrifice my affection to relatives and friends, and go where God, in his Providence, shall see fit to place me."[77]

Ann's father said yes, and so did she. In a way, Ann, her father, and Adoniram were all saying the same thing to God in different ways: "Here am I; bury me."

Two weeks after their wedding, they were on a ship bound for India. The voyage would last four months, and it would create problems with their Congregationalist supporters back home, as well as their families.

During their voyage, they spent a lot of time studying the Word on subjects related to planting churches. Their study led them to the conclusion that salvation should precede baptism by the church and that baptism, literally translated and applied, could only mean immersion.

They changed their entire view and affiliation. This was no small thing. They had departed America as Congregationalists, but they arrived in India as Baptists and were baptized by immersion soon after landing.

There was no Baptist mission board back in America to support them financially. But they resigned from the Congregationalist board, trusted God, and never looked back. Their willingness to confront their religious past, potentially upset their families, and lose all their financial support for the sake of biblical conviction reveals a lot about the mettle of their character and the tenacity of their convictions.

Fortunately, when news reached America of their changed position, Baptist churches rallied and created the American Baptist Missionary Union, which promptly began supporting them.

Labors and Trials in Burma

There were other changes ahead for the Judsons. They had to move several times after arriving in India. Eventually, they settled in Rangoon, Burma.

There they spent the next ten years attempting to learn the Burmese language—without a grammar, without a dictionary, without an English-speaking teacher, and without a church.

Adoniram learned by creating his own Burmese grammar over the next few years. In fact, it would take six years before he was able to preach his first sermon and to lead the first Burmese individual to faith in Jesus Christ.

In Burma, converting from Buddhism was punishable by death. It's little wonder that it took Judson twelve years of labor before he had eighteen people as baptized believers.

The kingdom of darkness seemed to take special note of Judson's work. On one occasion, Adoniram and another missionary traveled to see the emperor of Burma to petition for freedom to preach the gospel openly and without the threat of persecution or death for their converts. The emperor not only disregarded their request, but he also threw the gospel tract he'd been handed to the ground after reading only a few lines.

Adoniram and Ann encountered other trials as well. In addition to a stillborn child earlier, their son, Roger William Judson, died at eight months of age.

Ann Judson continued to serve faithfully along with her husband. She befriended the wife of the political leader of Rangoon and began to make some inroads.

Before long, a printing press arrived, and materials Adoniram had translated into Burmese were printed by the thousands. These included copies of Judson's translation of the Gospel of Matthew. Eventually, he would complete the translation of the entire New Testament into Burmese.

When war broke out between England and Burma in 1824, all the English missionaries were immediately suspected of serving the British government as spies. Most of the Burmese did not distinguish English-speaking American missionaries like the Judsons from the British.

On June 8, 1824, five years after they baptized their first convert, Burmese officials broke into the Judson home, tied up Adoniram, dragged him from his wife's side, and put him into prison.

He was placed in a prison building with other inmates. All lay on the floor, their feet in stocks and iron chains weighing fourteen pounds. He would wear the scars of those chains for the rest of his life. At night, a bamboo pole was passed between the prisoners' shackled feet and hoisted up by pulleys so that they literally hung upside down at a height that allowed only their heads and shoulders to rest on the ground.

After some time, Adoniram was moved to a cage that once housed a lion. It was neither high enough for him to stand up nor broad enough for him to lie down.

During this time, Ann delivered their daughter Maria and would walk with her every day, bringing food to the prison and begging the jailer to pass it along to Adoniram. But soon Ann became ill and unable to nurse her baby. The jailer had mercy on them and actually let Adoniram take the baby out into the village each day and beg for some nursing mother to give the child milk.[78]

Finally, and suddenly, Adoniram was released after seventeen months in prison. He was needed to interpret between British and Burmese officials negotiating a peace treaty.

Less than a year after his return home, Ann was dead. A few months later, their little daughter Maria died. Three months after that, he received news that his father had recently died as well.

Adoniram was crushed. He entered a deep depression that would last some three years. He eventually dropped his translation work. He retreated from anything that might promote a sense of happiness or pleasure. He stopped eating with the other missionaries at the mission house. He renounced his honorary Doctor of Divinity degree Brown University had given him. He gave away all his savings to the Baptist Mission Board and asked that his salary be reduced.

He then built a hut some distance from the mission house, deep in the jungle where he could be alone. He even dug an open grave beside his hut, where he would sit there for hours, even in pouring rain, contemplating his own death.

Judson expressed in a letter his feelings of utter spiritual desolation: "God is to me the great Unknown. I believe in him, but I find him not."[79]

He subsisted on a little rice each day and spent the day reflecting and praying for some sign that God had indeed forgiven him for all sorts of imagined failures: for not living up to his calling, for not being a humbler missionary, for getting caught up with pride in his commitment, for accepting any accolade from others.

The turning point came when he received a letter informing him that his brother, Elnathan, had died at the age of thirty-five. Ironically, this became his first step out of depression because Adoniram had prayed for many years for his brother's salvation, and the letter informed him that Elnathan had trusted Jesus Christ for his salvation and had died a believer.

He began to pour over the Scriptures again, and his tortured soul and mind began to receive hope in the promises of God's forgiveness and grace. He reentered the mission and picked up on his translation work. It was then, in 1831, that Judson noticed a new and growing interest in Christ among the Burmese people that he had never seen before.

Perhaps he, the seed, had truly died and been buried, alone. And now, by the refreshing work of God's Spirit, a great harvest was beginning.

An Expanding Ministry

Eight years after Ann's death, Adoniram married Sarah Boardman, the widow of a longtime missionary in Burma. The couple had several children, and as his family grew, so did the church.

In September 1835, Adoniram completed the Old Testament translation of the Bible into Burmese. He also baptized the one hundredth member of the Burmese church. These had been two of his goals, and they were now accomplished.[80]

Adoniram began a ministry to the Karen people, a large ethnic group in Burma. The Karen were pagan, but, amazingly, among the "traditions of the elders" that had been handed down for centuries was the story of a Creator God who made the first man and woman and placed them in a garden. There they were tempted by a serpent into sinning. Their ancient traditions also spoke of a coming deliverer and of a messenger who would bring news of the deliverer from a sacred parchment roll.[81]

And here came Adoniram Judson. Whereas he had once spent years sitting in a hut, praying that someone would accept his invitation to listen to the gospel, now in one winter alone, six thousand people came to him for material.

Some would travel three months from the borders of China and arrive saying, "Sir, we hear that there is an eternal hell; we are afraid of it; do give us a writing that will tell us how to escape it." Others came from the north, saying, "We have seen a writing that tells of an eternal God. Are you the man who gives away such writing? If so, pray give us one, for we want to know the truth before we die."[82]

New believers were being baptized. The buried seed was now bearing a harvest of fruit.

Later Life and Spiritual Legacy

Due to Sarah's declining health, they decided to return to the United States with their three oldest children to recover and raise awareness of the mission. Sarah died en route to America and was buried on an island. Adoniram and the children continued on.

When they arrived in Boston, Adoniram was greeted as a celebrity. Newspapers covered his arrival and every move. Everyone wanted to meet the first American missionary to return with stories of distant lands, prison shackles, disease, danger, suffering, and death.

Since Adoniram was actually suffering at the time with lung problems, he could only talk in a whisper, so an assistant relayed his words to his audiences. In addition, he hadn't spoken English for nearly twenty years, and he had a hard time putting three sentences together properly. In fact, he had written to his board before his arrival, saying, "Do not expect me to make public addresses, for in order to become an acceptable and eloquent preacher in a foreign language, I deliberately abandoned my own."[83]

Congregations and gatherings in America also were somewhat disappointed that instead of talking about his adventures, he most often simply wanted to whisper the gospel and talk about Christ. He had truly died to self.

While in America, Adoniram met Emily Chubbock, a woman with a rather well-known literary career underway. They fell in love, and she agreed to be his wife, leaving her career and the comforts of home for 108-degree weather, disease, and difficulty. She became one more seed who said, "Here I am, Lord; bury me."

In 1846, now accompanied by Emily, Adoniram returned to Burma and continued the work there. After several more years of fruitful ministry, his health began to fail.

When he had arrived in Burma in his twenties, he had hoped and prayed for one hundred believers and one church. Sometime after his death, at the age of 61, a survey reported over 200,000 Christians and hundreds of churches in Burma. One out of every 58 Burmese citizens had come to faith in Christ.[84]

Since his death, every Burmese dictionary and grammar has been based on the original work of Adoniram Judson. His Bible is still the premier translation for the Burmese people.

LEGACIES OF LIGHT

On the day he baptized his first convert, a day he'd waited some six years to see, he wrote in his journal, "Oh, may [this baptism] prove to be the beginning of a series of baptisms in the Burman empire which shall continue in uninterrupted success to the end of the age."[85]

Today, the fruit continues. There are nearly 4,000 evangelical Baptist congregations, which include some 1.9 million people and counting.[86] And they all trace their spiritual lineage to Adoniram Judson.

On April 3, 1850, Adoniram boarded a ship for a voyage he hoped would help him recover his strength. Instead, he became terribly ill, and eight days into the voyage, he passed away.

That evening the crew gathered in silence. After a few words by the unbelieving captain, Judson's body was lowered into the Indian Ocean, without even a prayer.[87]

That wouldn't have mattered to Adoniram Judson. He had died long before—a seed, a kernel of wheat, surrendered, sacrificed, and buried but still bearing fruit. His welcome to heaven by his Savior would have been amazing to see.

So many truths are illustrated by this man's life. Here are two important ones we need to keep in mind:

* Serving Christ does not eliminate potential suffering, and it may actually increase it.
* Willingness to suffer brings one to the threshold of spiritual fruit, and if one perseveres, such fruit is certain.

No matter where we have been placed in ministry, we can expect suffering, but as we persevere, we can also expect God to use our suffering for His glory. Let us say, in effect, "Here am I, Lord; bury me."

On a marble slab outside a Baptist church in the town where he was born are engraved the following words, which I believe are all that Adoniram Judson would care to have said about him:

> Rev. Adoniram Judson
> Born August 9, 1788
> Died April 12, 1850
> Malden his birthplace.
> The ocean, his sepulchre.
> Converted Burmans
> And the Burmese Bible
> His monument.
> His record is on high.

FANNY CROSBY

Travel back in Israel to the early centuries, and you would discover one particular handicap so feared that it was always associated with the wrath of God. What was this malady? Blindness.

Aristotle mentioned that in the Mediterranean region, blindness was believed to be hereditary, the result of someone in the family tree being blind.[88] We can easily imagine how people would refuse to marry someone even remotely related to a blind person because they were terrified that it would somehow be inherited or passed along.

In addition, blindness was considered irreversible. So, when Jesus Christ appeared in this region, blindness was considered by everyone to be incurable—unless, of course, God miraculously cured it.[89]

A Blind Man Healed

With that context in mind, let's turn to John 9. Knowing the contemporary attitude toward blindness helps us understand why the disciples asked the question and why Jesus responded as He did.

Verse 1 says, "As He [Jesus] passed by, He saw a man blind from birth." This was a grown man who had never been able to see. His was the most hopeless case imaginable. His blindness clearly was incurable.

Jesus' disciples then asked Him, "Who sinned, this man or his parents, that he would be born bind?" (verse 2). The disciples had simply bought the religious answer to disabilities: somebody had sinned; somebody was at fault.

Obviously, disabilities can result from any number of things—poor medical care; drugs, alcohol, or disease introduced prenatally; accidents; and genetic disorders. But even these things are, according to a correct understanding of Scripture, secondary causes of God's sovereign purpose.

In other words, God doesn't say, "Well, just look at what your mother did while she was pregnant," or "Look at what the doctor did (or didn't do) when you were born." God never says to you or me, "That particular event was out of My control. I'm sorry it happened, but there was nothing I could do about it."

That was the prevalent view in the first century, and the idea persists even into this twenty-first century: "Somebody did something wrong, and now some other person has to pay for it for the rest of his or her life." God had nothing to do with it. Somebody sinned.

Now look at Jesus' answer in verse 3: "It was neither that this man sinned, nor his parents; but it was so that the works of God might be displayed in him."

That was shocking news. Even today, Jesus' answer is alarming—yet also comforting. God was behind this man's disability. Jesus was saying that everything is ultimately secondary to God's purposes, which are primary.

Jesus Christ stunned His disciples by declaring that this man's lifelong disability was actually planned by God to bring glory to Him and credibility to the gospel at this moment in time. And this would be accomplished through what Jesus was about to do—namely, turn this disabled man into a passionate, fearless, evangelist by miraculously giving him sight.

We are told Jesus "spat on the ground, and made clay of the spittle, and applied the clay to his eyes, and said to him, 'Go, wash in the pool of Siloam'" (verses 6-7). We're also told later that He did this on a Sabbath day (verse 14).

What's all this about spitting on the ground and making mud? Why didn't He just command this man to see? All sorts of fanciful and allegorical interpretations have been read into what Jesus did here. Oh, it must mean Jesus was metaphorically going back to the garden. He was going to make the blind man a new man, like Adam, out of the dust of the ground. Just as God breathed on Adam, so the spittle comes from the mouth of Christ, and on and on. That all sounds very interesting, and it might sell some study guides one day, but it misses the point.

Jesus Christ, who knows the future, knew that He would use this blind man to confound the religious leaders, the Pharisees. So, the first thing Jesus did was violate their rules of Sabbath keeping. Instead of simply speaking so that this man was healed, He did what they would have considered physical labor. He made some mud.

The rabbis had defined Sabbath rest so ridiculously that it meant a man couldn't carry a handkerchief in his hand from an upstairs room to a downstairs room; he couldn't light a lamp or put out a lamp on the Sabbath. He couldn't cut his fingernails or pull a stray hair out of his beard.[90] In fact, women weren't even allowed to look in a mirror on the Sabbath because they would be tempted to fix something, which would constitute work.

It's very clear that Jesus intentionally set up this conflict with the Pharisees.

Furthermore, by making mud, Jesus was applying a poultice to the man's eyelids. Again, the Jewish leaders didn't allow any medical work on the Sabbath unless it was necessary to save someone's life. They didn't even allow one to treat a toothache or pour cold water on a sprained ankle.[91]

In curing this man Jesus was intentionally breaking the traditions of the religious leaders, which meant absolutely nothing to God. He was working with His hands and applying what would be perceived as medical treatment. Notice, too, that Jesus prescribed a further remedy by telling the man to go and wash himself off in the pool of Siloam.

In other words, Jesus deliberately set up this conflict so that the religious leaders would be boxed into a corner. They would have to either rethink their religious traditions or deny what was obviously a work of God. They believed and taught that blindness could be cured only by the hand of God, so Jesus' healing this man must mean He is God incarnate or at least empowered by God.

When Jesus miraculously gave this man sight, the man then engaged the religious leaders with fearless courage in two different conversations. The crux of his defense of Christ boils down to verses 32-33, where he said, "Since the beginning of time it has never been heard that anyone opened the eyes of a person born blind. If this man were not from God, He could do nothing."

It was obvious to the formerly blind man, as it should have been to everyone present, that the One who healed him was from God.

His was an irrefutable testimony to the power of God through Jesus Christ, the Son of Man.

The Pharisees had nothing to say! The only thing they could do was call the man a sinner and expel him from the synagogue (verse 34).

Think of this. God allowed this man to suffer his entire life so that at that moment, he could establish a witness to the authenticity of the divine power of Jesus Christ. This man's disability was planned—it was purposed by God.

Forget the fact that he was healed. One day every believer will be healed. But God planned for this man to live the majority of his life blind. Why? It was not because he had sinned or because his parents had sinned; it was so that "the works of God might be displayed in him."

A Gifted Blind Woman

Believers who live with disabilities yet to be cured testify to the divine power and grace of Jesus Christ and become incredible, convicting witnesses to the work of God displayed through them.

Perhaps the most prolific musical testimony in the history of the Christian church was a blind woman who testified courageously of her salvation, writing,

And I shall see Him face to face,

And tell the story—saved by grace.

The words of this hymn ("Saved by Grace") and 8,000 others she wrote have been printed more than 100 million times in numerous languages. In fact, she wrote under 200 different pen names because hymnal publishers didn't want people to know she had entirely dominated their hymnals.

She would have as many as forty hymns churning away before writing them down. In reality, she never really wrote any of them down, because she was blind. She dictated them to an assistant who wrote them down.

Her name was Frances Jane Crosby. She was most commonly known as Fanny Crosby.

Fanny wasn't born blind. When she was six weeks old, she caught a cold. The family physician was away at the time, and a country doctor was called to treat her. He prescribed hot mustard poultices to be applied to her eyelids, which had become swollen and inflamed with some sort of rash. The infection cleared up, but the treatment scarred her eyes, and soon her parents realized she had lost her sight.

It was later discovered that this particular doctor was not

even qualified to practice medicine. He left town in a hurry and was never heard of again.

When she was five years old, friends and neighbors pooled their funds to send Fanny and her mother to see the best eye specialist in the country, Dr. Valentine Mott. She never forgot his diagnosis and his words to her: "Poor child, I am afraid you will never see again."[92]

She refused to be discouraged. In fact, the first poem she composed, when she was only eight years old, goes like this:

> Oh, what a happy soul I am,
> Although I cannot see!
> I am resolved that in this world
> Contented I will be.
> How many blessings I enjoy
> That other people don't,
> To weep or sigh because I'm blind
> I cannot, and I won't![93]

Fanny would later write, "If I could meet that doctor now, I would say, 'Thank you, for making me blind. It [was] intended by the blessed providence of God that I should be blind all my life and I thank God for the [way He arranged it]."[94]

In these words we find a proper balance. The secondary cause might be a doctor unqualified to practice medicine, but the primary cause is the intentional plan and providence of God so that His work and His glory might be put on display.

One ability God clearly gave Fanny—and it was displayed early on—was a near photographic memory. A neighbor took Fanny under her wing and taught her the Bible. By the time she was ten years old, Fanny could quote Genesis, Exodus, Leviticus, Numbers, Deuteronomy, the book of Proverbs, and most of the Psalms, as well as Matthew, Mark, Luke, and John.

It was obvious that Fanny was capable of a formal education, so her mother enrolled her in New York City's famous Institution for the Blind. She loved every subject—except mathematics. She even wrote a little poem to voice her frustration:

> I loathe, abhor, it makes me sick,
> To hear the word Arithmetic![95]

After she graduated, she went on to become one of the institution's most famous teachers. In total, she was at the school for twenty-three years.

Fanny soon became famous for writing poetry and secular songs. She even wrote the first secular cantata by an American composer, called *The Flower Queen*. Three books of her poems were published.

She was incredibly passionate about politics too; in fact, she knew at least five presidents personally, and she lobbied in Washington for the education of the blind. She was the first woman ever to address Congress, urging them through poetic lines to support the education of the blind.

During the Civil War, she often pinned a miniature Union Flag to her dress to show her support for Abraham Lincoln. On one occasion, in a restaurant, a woman from the south found this offensive and snapped at her to take that "dirty rag" off. Fanny jumped to her feet and said, "Repeat that remark at your peril." The restaurant manager arrived in time to prevent a fight.[96]

A New Direction

Although Fanny Crosby knew much of the Bible by heart, she didn't know the Savior until she was thirty years old. She was attending a revival service in New York City. After the sermon and a prayer, the congregation began singing Isaac Watts's great hymn, "Alas! And Did My Savior Bleed?" When they reached the last stanza and the words "Here, Lord, I give myself away, 'til all that I can do," she gave her life to Christ.[97]

Up to this point Fanny had yet to write one sacred hymn. She had written music that was sung by minstrels on city stages and published secular volumes of poetry—but not one hymn.

In fact, it would be more than ten years before she wrote her first hymn. That came about as a result of meeting William Bradbury, the famous hymn writer and publisher, who challenged her to write for the gospel's sake—to use her talents for Christ. On the spot, she agreed and within a matter of days sent her first hymn text to him for publication. She was forty years of age. She would go on to write more than 8,000 hymns over the course of the next 51 years.

Fanny's personal prayer was that her music would be instrumental in leading a million people to faith in Jesus Christ. I have little doubt that prayer was answered.

Ira D. Sankey, who sang for D. L. Moody, began singing her songs in their revival meetings. A hundred years later, George Beverly Shea and Cliff Barrows would sing her songs in Billy Graham crusades. She came to faith in Christ at the singing of a hymn, and God in turn used the singing of her hymns to display His glory and, no doubt, bring many to faith in Christ.

Some Abiding Lessons

I want to pull from Fanny Crosby's life and ministry three important principles or lessons for all of us.

Usability in One Area of Life Is Often Created when We Accept Our Inability in Other Areas of Life

What makes Fanny Crosby's testimony so compelling is her submission to an incredibly difficult life. She accepted her blindness with joyful submission to the providence of God.

Frankly, she, like many others, remains a challenge for us today. So many of us are tempted to spend our lives pining away over doors the Lord has bolted shut instead of looking for doors the Lord has already opened.

Instead of developing resentment or resignation, Fanny rejoiced that the work of God and His glory could be displayed in and through her.

Victory over One Issue of Suffering Doesn't Guarantee Victory over Every Issue

Again, the study of someone's life not only highlights the person's successes but also reveals some failures.

Fanny married a former student, Alexander van Alstyne, who had also enrolled at the New York Institution for the Blind. They got to know each other over the course of several years and fell in love. Van, as he was known, became an outstanding organist.

A year after their marriage, they had their only child, a daughter they named Frances. Sadly, not long after her birth, she died, perhaps from typhoid fever. Van grew more and more reclusive in his grief. And Fanny herself never spoke publicly about being a mother until near the end of her life, when she opened up about her years of sorrow.

Eventually, after years of living together intermittently, Fanny and Van separated. Most biographers and historians conclude that this was the result of Van's inability to cope with the sorrow of losing his little girl.

For both Fanny and Van, it was one thing to deal with the disability of blindness, but it was almost too much to deal with the grief of death. Many believe Fanny's hymn "Safe in the Arms of Jesus" was inspired by her daughter's death.

Fanny spent the last twenty years of her life, supported

by appreciative benefactors as she composed hymn after hymn that spoke of longing for heaven.

Disability Is Ultimately in the Hand of Our Sovereign Lord, Both as to Its Cause and Its Cure

A disability should be our testimony that the grace of God and the trustworthiness of Jesus are sufficient, even during the deepest trials.

Frankly, suffering is the universal language of the human race. All of us suffer somewhere, somehow, to some extent. Why? So that as we demonstrate trust in the grace and purposes of God, *the work of God might be displayed through us*.

We are each a sheet of music upon which a perfect, loving, intentionally creative Lord is composing the harmony of His glory and His grace. And one day—one day—the tables will be turned, and those who have suffered most will sing the loudest.

Those of us who see should never think that seeing the Father's house will mean the same thing to us in the same way as it will to someone who was blind. Likewise, we should not think for a moment that walking down golden streets beside the River of Life and kneeling at the feet of Jesus will be quite the same for us who take these abilities for granted as it will be for someone who can't walk or kneel or speak.

I think God in His grace typically—not always but typically—gradually takes away our physical and mental abilities over time to make us both long for heaven all the more and then enjoy it even more when we get there. And those of us who even now are dealing with disabilities and experiencing suffering and sorrow are, according to God's unique plan, a display of the glory and grace of God.

Fanny Crosby died at the age of ninety-four, having displayed the work of God through her life. Near the end of her life she said these words:

> *I have always believed that the good Lord, in His infinite mercy, by this means [blindness] consecrated me to the work that I am still permitted to do. When I remember how I have been so blessed, how can I [complain]?[98]*

It is little wonder that on her memorial headstone are words from what may be her most famous hymn, "Blessed Assurance." The lyrics reflect her trust in Christ, which caused her to live and write with such confidence and joy and the assurance of that coming day she has since gone on to celebrate.

> Blessed assurance, Jesus is mine!
> O what a foretaste of glory divine!
> Heir of salvation, purchase of God,
> Born of His Spirit, washed in His blood.
>
> This is my story, this is my song,
> Praising my Savior, all the day long;
> This is my story, this is my song,
> Praising my Savior, all the day long.

JIM AND ELISABETH ELLIOT

One of the misconceptions of the Christian life is that we should be surrounded by peacetime conditions—that somehow we can avoid the war of the ages, the conflict that rages around us for human lives and eternal souls.

According to God's design, however, every Christian has been drafted into service. In fact, we've all been commissioned to take the gospel to a world at war with God. There are thousands of different specific assignments, according to the will of God for our individual lives, but we have all been commissioned into this service by our victorious General.

The apostle Paul speaks of our special commissioning in 2 Corinthians 5:18: "Now all these things are from God, who reconciled us to Himself through Christ and gave us the ministry of reconciliation." Our ministry is that of reconciliation. In other words, our lives are to serve as front parlors, where we demonstrate the gospel of Christ and present it to those engaged in war against their Creator.

Paul goes on in verse 19 to describe this reconciliation: "Namely, that God was in Christ reconciling the world to Himself, not counting their trespasses against them, and He has committed to us the word [the *logos*, the message] of reconciliation."

Mankind is reconciled to God by means of Christ's death, burial, and resurrection. Christ, the Son of God, has paid for our trespasses against His holy character. Those sins no longer stand in the way of making peace with God, of signing the peace treaty with Him.

Reconciliation involves accepting the terms of surrender

offered by God through the peace treaty drafted by Christ on the cross. We surrender to the truth that He alone is God, that Christ alone can save us, and that we are sinners in need of a Savior. This is our message, and this is our ministry.

And in case any of the Corinthian believers—or any of us—get the idea that this ministry and message is for a special group called the clergy, Paul emphasizes that we are all "ambassadors for Christ, as though God were making an appeal through us" (verse 20). As Christ's ambassadors, we are to be begging the world to "be reconciled to God," to come into the parlor, so to speak, and sign the peace treaty God has established through the death of Christ on the cross.

Part of the problem we have in understanding our commission is that we frequently misunderstand this concept of an ambassador. We tend to think in terms of modern-day ambassadors spending time in lavish hotels, attending banquets, wearing tuxedos or dinner gowns, and nodding and smiling at foreign dignitaries who really don't mean what they say.

When Paul wrote this letter to the Corinthians, Roman provinces were divided into two types. Senatorial provinces were peaceful regions that had no need for a large military force to be stationed there.

Imperial provinces were more turbulent. They were on the frontiers of the empire and recently conquered. A large military force would be stationed in these provinces.

Ambassadors —and there were always more than one— assigned to imperial provinces were there to deliver the terms of peace. They determined the boundaries of the new province and drew up a constitution for its new administration. They were literally responsible for bringing these people into the family of the Roman Empire.[99]

Consider these characteristics of ambassadors:

They spend their lives among people who often speak a different language with different traditions and a different way of life.

Ambassadors deliver a definite message and carry out a definite policy, but they are to be alert for opportunities, study individuals, and cast about for methods to place before their hearers in the most attractive form possible the message from their own country and ruler.

Furthermore, it is the great responsibility of the ambassador to commend his country to the people amongst whom he is set.[100]

It is easy to imagine that Rome's first-century ambassadors would not have been appreciated, welcomed, or accepted and certainly would never be viewed as one of the tribe. The ambassador's goal was never to fully assimilate into that country but to consistently represent his own country—to speak highly of the kingdom to whom this vanquished people must surrender. Throughout the history of the Roman Empire, many ambassadors lost their lives.

The Cost of Being Christ's Ambassadors

Certainly, throughout the history of the Christian church, those who have gone to provinces far and wide on behalf of the kingdom of Christ have often lost their lives. Martyrs for the gospel are not diminishing even in our day. Conservative estimates by missions agencies place the number of Christian martyrs at about 176,000 per year! That's 482 a day, or one every three minutes.

Most of these deaths will never make it into the news; they will be kept out of the spotlight. But make no mistake, these martyrs will be received into heaven's glory and given a special crown (Revelation 2:10).

The deaths of five New Tribes missionaries never made it into the headlines.[101] They were attempting to reach a savage tribe in Bolivia in 1943 when they were killed.

Thirteen years later, the martyrdom of five missionaries gained greater publicity when *Life* magazine published a ten-page article on their mission and their deaths. This event sent ripples through the Christian community, as God used their deaths to move the church to send thousands of new missionaries into service.

The names of those five martyrs were Roger Youderian, Pete Fleming, Ed McCully, Nate Saint, and Jim Elliot. Elliot became the best-known among them, primarily because his story was retold through two books written by his wife, Elisabeth, who eventually hosted an international radio program called *Gateway to Joy*.

Elisabeth, along with the older sister of Nate Saint, made contact with, and eventually went to live among, the Aucas,[102] the same vicious tribe who had killed their loved ones by spearing them on a sandy riverbank, deep in the jungles of Ecuador on January 8, 1956.

However, we need to back up a bit to learn how Jim and Elisabeth Elliot accepted their foreign commission as ambassadors for Christ. The two met at Wheaton College, where they were both majoring in Greek, preparing for some type of linguistic ministry to an unreached people group.

Elisabeth recounted:

> *There was a student on campus whom I had been noticing more and more. My brother Dave had been encouraging me to get acquainted with him. He and Dave were on the wrestling squad, so I went to a match—supposedly*

> *to watch my brother. I found myself laughing with the crowd at Jim Elliot—nicknamed, the "India-rubber man" because he could be tied in knots but could not be pinned to the mat.*
>
> *I noticed Jim in the Foreign Missionary Fellowship on campus—earnest, committed to missionary service, outspoken. I noticed him in dining hall lines with little white cards in his hand, memorizing Greek verbs or Scripture verses.*
>
> *Finally, my brother Dave invited Jim to come to our home for Christmas break, and we ended up having long, long talks after everyone else had gone to bed.*
>
> *When we returned back to college, I began to hope that he would sit next to me in class once in a while—and he did—often, even when at times he had to trip over other people to get the seat.[103]*

Eventually, Jim shared his heart's desire to marry her, but first he believed God wanted him to settle in Ecuador and learn the language of the people. Elisabeth also came to Ecuador to serve.

Jim and Elisabeth agreed to put off marriage until they had both learned the language. This was so that marriage and homemaking and parenting duties wouldn't interfere with their ability to communicate and they would be able to accomplish their ultimate desire to serve as ambassadors to these people.

Finally, five years after Jim proposed, Jim and Elisabeth were married in Ecuador.

Not long afterward, Jim and his four missionary teammates began to make contact with the Aucas. The Aucas were a brutal, primitive tribe who took pride in the number of men their men had speared to death.

Roger Youderian, Ed McCully, Pete Fleming, and their pilot Nate Saint, along with Jim Elliot, spent months pouring over maps of the Ecuadorian jungle. They were very aware of the earlier attempt to reach a savage tribe in Bolivia, which had resulted in the five New Tribes missionaries being killed.

They were not pursuing their goal on a whim. They knew what they were risking. But they firmly believed this was their calling—to be ambassadors for Christ—even if it meant losing their lives.

The missionaries began flying over an Auca village, dropping gifts for the natives. They rigged a loud speaker to the plane, and as they flew over, they would shout out, "We are your friends," using Auca words they had learned.

The team found a sandbar along the nearby river, where they landed their plane. Eventually contact was made with some members of the tribe. Everything was progressing wonderfully, and the missionary team was excited.

On January 8, 1956, Nate Saint flew over the village. When he spotted nearly a dozen warriors on the trail leading to their river landing, he returned to the sandbar and joined his teammates.

Within minutes the Aucas arrived, and the killing began. Even though all the missionaries were armed, they had decided not to use any of their weapons against the Aucas, even if they were being attacked. They knew that while they were ready for heaven, the Aucas were not.[104]

Steve Saint, years later, was seated at a campfire with several of these warriors, now believers and committed disciples of Christ. For the first time ever, they recounted to Steve the events of that afternoon. They remembered being mystified as to why the missionaries didn't fire their weapons at them but into the air instead. Why did one missionary simply wait for one of the warriors to wade out in the river to spear him? One of the men said to Steve, "If he had fled just a little, surely he would have lived."[105]

Months after the killings, Elisabeth Elliot, her young daughter, and Rachel Saint, Steve's aunt, were able to establish a home among the Aucas, thanks to a young native girl who had fled, come to faith in Christ, and now led the women back to her village.

These women lived among them, adapting to the hardships of such a primitive life in order to deliver the gospel to the people. Rachel translated the Scriptures into their language, and Elisabeth personally led to Christ two of the warriors who had martyred her husband and the other missionaries that fateful afternoon.

Elisabeth later remembered,

> *When I stood by my short-wave radio in the jungle of Ecuador and heard that my husband was missing, God brought to my mind the words of Isaiah the prophet, "When you pass through the waters, I will be with you." . . . Jim's absence thrust me, forced me, hurried me to God, my hope and my only refuge. . . . I can say to you that suffering is an irreplaceable medium through which I learned an indispensable truth. I Am. I am the Lord. In other words, that God is God.[106]*

Nine years after the martyrdom of the five men, the Gospel of Mark was published in the Auca language. A church had already been established, and the pastor of the church was one of the warriors in that killing party. His name was Kimo, and he would, amazingly enough, personally baptize Steve Saint, Nate's son, in that river.

That's the ministry of reconciliation. One author wrote, "God had used these women, a wife and sister of the slain missionaries, to reconcile with the Aucas and bring them the ultimate reconciliation of Christ's salvation."[107]

Steve Saint and his family moved to Ecuador in 1995 to build an airport and a hospital for the tribes of this region, including the Aucas.

Steve published the conversation he had with the now aged Auca warriors who had taken part in the killing of Jim Elliott and Steve's own father. One of the warriors told a story that was confirmed by several other warriors and women who had been there on the sandy riverbank that afternoon some forty years earlier.

They talked about hearing music, strange music. As the missionaries lay on that riverbank dead or dying, their killers began to hear music and looked above the tree line to see a multitude of *cowodi*, their word for missionary or foreigner.

One native described this singing choir as lights, moving around and shining, a sky full of jungle beetles similar to fireflies, with a light that was brighter and didn't blink on and off.

One of the women who was there told Steve Saint she had hidden in the bush during the attack, and after it was over, she saw *cowodi* above the trees, singing. She said, "We didn't know what this kind of music was until we later heard recordings played by Rachel Saint . . . recordings of choir music."

Steve said, "Apparently all the participants saw this bright multitude in the sky and knew they should be afraid, because they knew it was something supernatural."[108]

Without a doubt, there at that river that day, an angelic host had arrived to testify that these ambassadors were heading home. As they were taken from their assigned post on earth to their home country of heaven, they were being welcomed by an angelic choir.

God rarely does something like that. Perhaps He does it just enough to give tangible evidence that Christ has overcome the world—even when His ambassadors lay dying on a sandy riverbank.

We are His ambassadors. We have been given the honor to represent His everlasting kingdom, delivering to our world the terms of surrender and peace with God.

This is our ministry. This is our message. We are His ambassadors; we are His messengers of reconciliation.

May the Spirit of God enable us to see beyond the details, to see beyond the normal duties of life to another kingdom, which we represent in private and in public.

HUDSON TAYLOR

Hudson Taylor was born into a loving, committed Christian family. Yet, even though he was taught the Bible and was knowledgeable of basic doctrine, he remained personally skeptical.

When he was fifteen years of age, he landed a job at a city bank, where he was surrounded by young men who made fun of his family's old-fashioned religious ideas. That experience began to cement his unbelief.

In the providence of God, however, Hudson developed a problem with his eyesight. The problem lasted only a brief time, but it was long enough for him to lose his job at the bank.

By the time he turned seventeen, his thirteen-year-old sister had committed to praying for his salvation three times a day, though Hudson was unaware of this. He was also unaware that his mother had excused herself from an appointment with friends one afternoon to privately pray.

That same afternoon, Hudson found himself at home. He later wrote:

> *I had a holiday, and in the afternoon looked through my father's library to find some book with which to while away the unoccupied hours. Nothing attracting me, I turned over a basket of pamphlets and selected from amongst them a Gospel tract that looked interesting, saying to myself: "There will be a story at the commencement and a sermon or moral at the close. I will take the [story] and leave the [sermon] for those who like it." ...*
>
> *While reading [the pamphlet] I . . . was struck with the phrase: "The finished work of Christ." "Why does this au-*

thor use this expression?" I questioned. "Why not say the atoning or propitiatory work of Christ?"

Immediately the words "It is finished" [John 19:30] suggested themselves to my mind.

"What was finished?"

And I at once replied, "A full and perfect atonement and satisfaction for sin. The debt was paid for our sins, and not for ours only, but also for the sins of the whole world."

Then came the further thought, "If the whole work was finished and the whole debt paid, what is there left for me to do?"

And with this dawned the joyful conviction, as light flashed into my soul by the Holy Spirit, that there was nothing in the world to be done but to fall down on one's knees and, accepting this Saviour and His salvation, praise Him for evermore.[109]

And that's exactly what Hudson Taylor did. The year was 1849. Within a year he began medical studies, hoping to serve as a missionary in the unreached land of China.

Faith and Faithfulness

In order to fully prepare for the hardships of missionary pioneering, Hudson moved into the slum district of London called Drainside. As the name itself suggests, it wasn't a comfortable place to live.

He found that he could live off porridge and bread most of the week, with meat occasionally. He used all his remaining money for medical supplies so that he could personally assist the poverty-stricken people in his neighborhood.

He wrote to his sister that he had one big problem though: the medical doctor he worked for often forgot to pay him his weekly salary. Hudson had to remind him every week, and it became so frustrating to Hudson that he finally decided to give it over to the Lord and trust Him to remind the doctor to pay him.

He believed that entrusting this to the Lord would be a good way to develop his faith. So, he stopped reminding the doctor—and the doctor stopped paying him. God didn't seem to be reminding him. Eventually, the rent came due, and Hudson had no money to pay it. His food was running out as well.

Still, he did not ask to be paid, and the doctor seemed to have no clue that he owed Hudson. At the end of the week, however, the doctor suddenly turned and said, "By the [way], Taylor, is not your salary due again?" Hudson wrote, "I had to swallow two or three times before I could answer.... I told him as quietly as I could that it was overdue some little time.

How thankful I felt at this moment! God surely had heard my prayer."

The doctor replied, "You know how busy I am. I wish I had thought of it a little sooner, for only this afternoon I sent all the money I had to the bank. Otherwise, I would have paid you at once."

That Saturday evening Hudson Taylor, feeling defeated and discouraged, was about to lock the clinic up when the doctor suddenly appeared, rather amused that one of his richest patients had just come by the doctor's home to pay his medical bill.

Hudson too was amused that such a wealthy client would come at 10:00 o'clock at night to pay a bill he could have paid anytime he wanted.

The doctor then gave Hudson a handful of banknotes and promised to pay him the balance he owed him the next week.

Hudson Taylor experienced incredible joy in this answered

prayer of faith.[110]

On another occasion, his boss was yet again behind in paying him. Hudson headed home discouraged and confused with the Lord. He had only one half-crown in his pocket for the weekend. In today's economy, that half-crown would be worth around ten to twelve dollars.

While ministering in Drainside Sunday evening, Hudson was met by a poor man who begged him to come and pray for his wife, who had only recently delivered a baby and neither she nor the newborn was doing well. Hudson reluctantly agreed to go, though he admitted later that he wasn't in the mood to help anybody that night.

When he arrived at the apartment, several starving children were huddled inside the bare dwelling, and a woman was lying on a cot in the corner with a newborn baby at her side, moaning. Clearly, both the woman and her child were malnourished—as was the entire family.

Hudson immediately knew that the Lord wanted him to give this family his half-crown, but his heart refused.

In a letter to his sister later, he shared the feelings he battled:

> *I began to tell them . . . they must not be cast down; that though their circumstances were very distressing there was a kind and loving Father in heaven. But something within me cried, "You hypocrite! Telling these unconverted people about a kind and loving Father in heaven, and not prepared yourself to trust Him without a half-crown." I was nearly choked [at the thought].[111]*

Hudson knelt down in that little room, and the battle raged in Taylor's heart as he began to pray. He wrote, "How I got through that form of prayer I know not, and whether the words uttered were connected or disconnected I cannot tell. . . . I put my hand into my pocket and slowly drawing out the half-crown, gave it to the man."[112]

Only then, did the joy of the Lord flood his heart. He knew this entire family would soon have food.

When he returned home, he ate his last bowl of porridge. Before going to bed, he got down on his knees and thanked the Lord that he had been empowered to give everything he had away. Then he reminded the Lord that he was out of both money and food.

The following day, a package without a return address or name arrived. The package contained a pair of winter gloves, and inside one of the gloves was four times the amount of money he had given away the night before.[113]

He would later write, "I cannot tell you how often my mind has recurred to this incident . . . If we are faithful to God in little things, we shall gain experience and strength that will be helpful to us in the more serious trials of life."[114]

Maybe that's where you are right now—learning to be faithful in the little things as God is working to deepen your faith and trust and prepare you for even greater challenges in the days ahead.

Ministry in China

Hudson Taylor sailed for China in 1853; he would spend fifty-one years serving in that country.

Soon after he arrived in China, he realized that his respect among the people and his acceptance as a religious teacher were being hindered by his Western apparel. His black overcoat earned him the nickname, "The Black Devil," and much of the taunting he encountered from young people had more to do with his strange apparel than the gospel he preached.

So, he went against all protocol and advice from others and decided to do something radical. He removed his Western clothing and put on the customary robe and slippers of a Chinese tutor. He even shaved the hair off his forehead to match the Chinese custom for teachers.

Hudson wrote his sister the rather shocking details that would create a scandal: "I had better tell you at once that on Thursday last at 11 p.m. I resigned my locks to the barber, dyed my hair a good black color, and in the morning had a proper queue or what we call a pigtail woven into [the back of my] own hair ... then, in Chinese dress, I set out."[115]

The reaction back in England was to be expected. He lost support without ever being contacted by his former supporters.

Hudson Taylor would eventually begin his own mission board, the China Inland Mission. And he would be known for his sensitivity toward Chinese culture and customs. His words to his missionary teammates are thought provoking: "Rude persons will seldom be out of hot water in China; and though earnest and clever and pious will not effect much. In nothing do we fail more, as a Mission, than in lack of tact and politeness."[116]

Hudson Taylor and his family suffered tremendously. His wife and several children died from diseases. He married again, only to experience the stillborn death of twin babies, a boy and a girl.

He and those who served with him were persecuted and often had to flee for their lives. He once commented that the China Inland Mission never established a missionary outpost without first surviving a riot—and they established more than three hundred mission stations. It's little wonder that his testimony influenced thousands of people to consider giving their lives in service to the Lord in another country.

Hudson Taylor was personally supported by Charles Spurgeon, C. I. Scofield, and D. L Moody. He often—and sometimes just in time—received financial gifts in the mail from his good friend George Mueller, who was enduring his own tests of faith and financial challenges in his ministry.

Hudson Taylor was known for his optimistic spirit. He credited this optimism to his confidence in the Lord. I have written down and often read and reread a statement he made: "If we are obeying the Lord, the responsibility rests with Him, not with us."[117]

Words of Wisdom

In a letter dated 1879, when Hudson Taylor was forty-seven years old and away from the mission, he wrote to the secretary of the mission, rehearsing several action points that would continue to give their ministry organizational health and effectiveness, along with spiritual vitality.

They were meant to be applied on an institutional level by the China Inland Mission, but they are equally applicable to all believers individually. I want to step away from a detailed biography at this point and comment on the five action points of Hudson Taylor, which, if observed, will give us all spiritual vitality and ministry effectiveness on both a personal and a team level.[118]

Improve the Character of the Work

Often what believers need is not to begin something new but to strengthen and improve what they are already doing.

On an organizational level, "this may involve new job descriptions, or establishing new reporting procedures and other lines of communication."[119]

In other words, self-evaluation and internal evaluation of any ministry organization is a healthy, though sometimes painful, process. But if it's worth doing, it's worth evaluating.

Howard Hendricks taught this same principle, when he spoke of "plussing." By this, he meant taking something you're doing that's worth doing and then doing it better . . . more efficiently . . . more effectively.

Deepen the Piety and Devotion

Paul wrote to Timothy, his son in the faith, "Discipline yourself for the purpose of godliness" (1 Timothy 4:7). That word "discipline" is a translation of the Greek *gumnazō* from which we get our word *gymnasium*. It literally means "exercise."

In other words, the apostle is saying that godly piety and devotion demand exercise. If you want to grow in godliness, you have to be willing to work up a spiritual sweat.

I remember years ago, we were at the beach with our girls. They were out in the water, and I told them to use our umbrella as their marker and stay in front of us. No matter how hard they tried, they drifted as each wave pushed them down the shoreline. The undertow would shift them farther and farther away. Sometimes they would literally get out of the water and run back up the beach to where we were and start over again.

What a picture this is of my life and yours. It's so easy to drift.

Every wave of demand, every pull of pressure, and the undertow of problems and challenges—perhaps even with some laziness and apathy thrown in—can cause us to drift without even realizing it.

We will never deepen our piety and devotion without intentional effort and a constant readjustment to the umbrella location of God's purpose and design.

Remove Stones of Stumbling, if Possible

Taylor was thinking of tough assignments that needed to be tackled. Some decisions need to be made, and obstacles to those decisions need to be overcome. But he also added, "if possible."

If possible. Some things just can't be changed. Some obstacles are not going to move until Jesus comes . . . you just have to deal with them. But wherever you can remove things that hinder your spiritual and ministry life, do it.

Hudson often reminded his missionary team that there are "three stages in work for God . . . first, *impossible*, then *difficult*, then *done*."[120] He didn't want missionaries joining the team who weren't willing to face challenges. In fact, all candidates who applied to the China Inland Mission were trained at the center they had set up in the slums of London. If they couldn't make it there, they weren't allowed to go to China.[121]

Oil the Wheels where They Stick

Hudson Taylor actually had in mind with this statement, personal relationships. He saw it as necessary to get out the oil can of love and apply it liberally to those relationships that just tend to stick. There is really no substitute for loving one another.

As an older man, he confided that one of his greatest challenges in missionary service was the trouble he had with the missionary family of the China Inland Mission. Thus, he pressed his entire staff to have well-oiled relationships.

Even still, he would often encourage himself and those around him by saying that things "will soon look up, with God's blessing, if looked after."[122]

What a balanced bond of perseverance and trust.

Supplement What Is Lacking

What Hudson Taylor means here is don't just point out the problem; supplement what's needed to fix it. Add whatever is lacking as you plan and carry out your plans for God.

These are wise words for churches, Christian organizations, and individual Christians: Improve the character of the work; deepen piety and devotion; remove stones of stumbling, if possible; oil the wheels where they stick; and supplement what is lacking.

A Legacy of Humble Service

One of the things Hudson Taylor was marked by was a sense of humility and, with it, a deep sense of joy—almost a sense of surprise—that God had chosen to use him for His glory.

He wrote, "I often think that God must have been looking for someone small enough and weak enough for Him to use ... and He found me."[123]

On one occasion, Hudson Taylor, the world-renowned missionary to China, was introduced as the guest speaker at a large church in Australia. The moderator of the service introduced the missionary in eloquent and glowing terms. He told the large congregation all that Taylor had accomplished in China and then presented him as "our illustrious guest." Taylor stood quietly for a moment and then said, "Dear Friends, I am merely the servant of an illustrious Master."[124]

In 1905, after having resigned as the head of the China Inland Mission, Hudson decided to take one last tour through some of his beloved cities and mission stations in China. During that tour, he passed away.

He was buried next to his first wife, Maria, in a small English cemetery in a village near a river. There is an interesting history regarding their gravesites.

Their graves were treated with utter disregard in China. In

fact, the cemetery was actually covered over by development in the 1960s and their grave markers destroyed.

However, in recent years those industrial buildings built over the cemetery were torn down, and Hudson and Maria's graves were found to be the only two graves in the cemetery still intact. In August 2013, their graves were moved to a local church where a memorial has been built to honor their lives.

In over 50 years of ministry, Hudson Taylor was responsible for leading nearly 1,000 missionaries into the vast country of China. Together they planted hundreds of churches and started and developed 125 schools. And more than 500 Chinese converts eventually joined the mission as staff members and volunteers.

The China Inland Mission became the largest Protestant missionary organization in the world.

Hudson Taylor learned to speak three different Chinese dialects, evangelized all eighteen provinces of the interior, and prepared a translation of the New Testament in the Ningbo dialect.

But if he were here today, I'm fairly confident he wouldn't care to hear any of that repeated. Rather, he would stress that he was simply the servant of an illustrious Master—someone small enough to be used by God and weak enough to be available for God to use.

He was struck with the truth of Christ's words on the cross —"It is finished!"—and he never got over the completed work of Christ on his behalf. And he never forgot that to Christ alone belongs all the glory, honor, and praise.

JOHN NEWTON

His nickname was "The Great Blasphemer" or "The African Blasphemer."

He was born in London, England, in 1725. His father was an unbelieving sea captain who commanded a prosperous trading ship. His mother was a godly woman who dedicated her life to training their only son. Her favorite source of curriculum was Isaac Watts's book entitled *Preservatives from the Sins and Follies of Youth*, and as a child, her son, John Newton, could quote and sing the songs of Watts that were written especially for children. One song began:

> Why should I join with those in play,
> In whom I've no delight;
> Who curse and swear but never pray;
> Who call ill names and fight?[125]

Tragedy struck early on, however, when at the age of seven, John Newton's mother died. And everything changed.

When John's father returned from his voyage, he remarried. His new wife didn't care for his young boy, so he was shipped off to boarding school, where a brutal headmaster made his life miserable.

A Seaman's Life

His father finally intervened and brought John on board his ship at the age of eleven. After several voyages and surrounded by ungodly influences, his mother's lessons were soon forgotten. By the time John turned sixteen, his profanity and wicked spirit equaled that of the sailors around him. He would write of those days, "I often saw the necessity of religion as a means of escaping hell; but I loved sin, and was unwilling to forsake it."[126]

When John was seventeen, his father decided he should sail to the West Indies and become involved in managing a Jamaican plantation owned by one of his friends. It was a plantation run by African slaves, and his father figured that over the next five years, John would make a small fortune managing the plantation.

But a week before he was to set sail, close friends of his deceased mother invited him to visit them. When John arrived, he immediately found a second home and a family—and the affection of a mother like the one he could barely remember.

The family's oldest daughter, Mary, was nearly fourteen, and John fell head over heels for her. He would write that she was kind and sweet and fun. She probably never knew his true feelings because he was struck dumb whenever she entered the room.

John so enjoyed his time with Mary and her family that he never mentioned leaving for Jamaica. In fact, he purposefully missed the deadline so that the ship sailed without him.

His father was furious, of course, and determined that John set sail on another ship, this one bound for Italy. During that voyage, for the first time without his father and in an incredibly pagan environment, his hatred for God deepened. At the same time, all he could think about was Mary.

Even though John hated religion and wanted nothing to do with God, the Lord protected John from many sins of the flesh. As the ship pulled into various ports and prostitutes were smuggled on board for the crew, John would climb the mast and hide out in the crow's nest high above.

When he returned to England after that year-long voyage, his father had another job waiting for him on yet another trading vessel. But John had a few days to go back to Mary's house to see her again and enjoy her family's hospitality.

Once again, he purposefully missed the deadline, and the ship sailed without him. Only this time, things didn't turn out so well. When he returned to London, his father again was furious with him. But while he waited for another job, he found himself in the wrong place at the wrong time.

The shipping industry in those days was primitive and dirty, and the treatment of the seamen was inhumane. But nothing was more inhumane than the Royal Navy. There were never enough volunteers to man the warships. So "press gangs" were sent out to capture young men and force them into naval service. John Newton fell victim to such a gang and was pressed into service.

He soon found himself working with condemned criminals from England's jails who had been given the choice of being hanged or serving on a British warship. The stench of the common quarters, ill-cooked food, the violence of his desperate companions, and the tyranny of the officers made life in the navy nearly unbearable for John.

When John's father found out what had happened, he wrote the ship's captain, who agreed to make John an officer. John's conditions immediately improved, and he actually began to enjoy this life at sea. He was as foulmouthed and atheistic as the unbelieving criminals and officers around him, but he still had one goal that never left his mind: he wanted to win the hand of Mary Catlett.

After a short voyage, John learned that his ship would be sailing to India and the East Indies and that he would be gone for the next five years. He had just one day's leave in which to see Mary again, to tell her of his love, and to ask her father for her hand in marriage. By now she was fifteen, and John was nineteen.

The visit was a disaster for John. Mary's father denied his request. He and his wife wanted their daughter marrying a man with better prospects. They even forbade John from ever visiting again or corresponding with Mary.

Mary herself seemed somewhat undecided, and John couldn't bear the thought of sailing away without knowing how she felt for him. In desperation, he jumped ship and deserted.

In a few days, he was captured and returned to his ship in shackles. Two days later, all 350 of the crew were assembled on deck to witness John Newton's flogging. He was given 96 lashes with a whip, a beating so brutal even one experienced member of the crew fainted.

He was stripped of his rank and humiliated—he knew Mary's parents would never reconsider now. Shackled below deck and filled with rage, he began planning a way to murder the captain and then throw himself overboard, committing suicide.

John would later write, "It was the secret hand of God that restrained me."[127]

Nineteen days later, they encountered the ship of a slave trader heading for the West Indies. The ship was in need of another crewmember, and John's captain gladly handed him over.

On board this ship, John gave full vent to his foul mouth, his insubordinate spirit, his hatred for God, and his love for tormenting anyone who seemed interested in religion. He also met a wealthy trader from West Africa who convinced John that the way to make his fortune and win Mary's hand was to follow in his footsteps.

John agreed and they disembarked at the man's plantation on an island just off the coast of West Africa. This man's mistress was an African woman who immediately decided she didn't like John Newton. John succumbed to fever and was unable to set sail with the merchant on his next voyage. He was left in the care of his partner's mistress, who had already decided to let him die.

In his journal John wrote:

> *I had not a little difficulty to procure a cup of water when burning with fever. My bed was a mat spread upon a board and a piece of wood was my pillow. Sometimes when she was in a good humor, she would send a slave to hand me her plate with whatever food was left on it after she had dined.*[128]

For a year he languished on that island—a slave to the slaves. He hated God all the more. He felt he had been abandoned and had no real reason to live.

He would later write that if it had not been for some of the chained slaves on that plantation taking pity on him and secretly giving him food of their own, he would have starved to death.

Turning Points

But then, shockingly, one day a ship anchored near his island after seeing some smoke, and some men came ashore asking the locals, "Have you heard of a white man named John Newton?" They had been sent by John's father.

It was 1747, and God was about to close in on the Great

Blasphemer.[129]

It took a year of business before the ship that rescued John, the *Greyhound*, made its way back to England. En route it encountered a storm so violent that it began to sink. John "worked the pumps from 3 in the morning until noon, slept for an hour, and then took the helm and steered the ship till midnight."[130]

Men and provisions had been swept into the sea. The rigging was torn, and the hold was full of water. The crew feared they would all die at sea.

Some of the men thought John was like Jonah to them. They threatened to throw him overboard to see if God would still the storm, but the captain didn't allow it.

In the midst of that storm, for the first time since he was a little boy, John Newton began to pray. He began to evaluate his life and his hatred and blasphemy of God. He thought of his mother and those early hymns of Isaac Watts.

He wrote later that he decided then and there to attempt to reform his life, to quit swearing and resolve to do better. Of course, this wasn't salvation; this was self-reformation. But John began reading a Bible he found, along with Christian literature. He had no Christian friend or Bible-believing pastor to talk to about the true gospel and saving faith in Christ alone. But God was at work.

The ship survived the journey and landed just off Ireland.

John's father had assumed the *Greyhound* had not survived the storm and that John was dead. But then he received a lengthy letter from his son, thanking him for sending people to look for him and informing him of the past few years' adventures. John even told his father about his love for Mary Catlett and his resolution to be a better man.

His father was thrilled. In fact, when John arrived back in London, he discovered that his father had gone to the Catletts to speak to Mary's father on John's behalf.

In the meantime, John was given another assignment on a slave-trading ship when he was twenty-three years of age. It was during that voyage—and another life-threatening fever—that John fully came to terms with his sin and trusted in Christ alone for forgiveness of his sins. He viewed this as his moment of true and genuine conversion to Jesus Christ.

Of the more than three hundred hymns John Newton would later write, one would become his personal testimony of salvation during this moment in his life. The lyrics read:

> In evil long I took delight
> Unawed by shame or fear,
> Till a new object struck my sight,
> And stopped my wild career.
>
> I saw One hanging on a tree,
> In agonies and blood,
> Who fixed his languid eyes on me,
> As near his cross I stood.
>
> Sure never, till my dying breath,
> Can I forget that look;
> It seemed to charge me with his death,
> Though not a word he spoke.
>
> My conscience felt and owned the guilt,
> And plunged me in despair;
> I saw my sins his blood had spilt,
> And helped to nail him there.
>
> Alas! I knew not what I did,

But now my tears are vain,
Where shall my trembling soul be hid?
For I the Lord have slain!

A second look he gave, which said –
"I freely all forgive;
This blood is for thy ransom paid,
I died, that thou mayest live."[131]

Less than two years later, John proposed to Mary Catlett, and she accepted. He was now twenty-five.

Almost immediately, John was given the command of a slave ship and soon after marrying his bride, he made two voyages. As a new Christian, he struggled with the slave trade, and he began keeping a detailed journal. That journal would become the earliest known document recording details of the slave trade, giving minute information about the conditions on board ship and the insurrections and suicides of slaves.[132]

John Newton would later meet William Wilberforce, and the two would become good friends. Wilberforce would use Newton's journal as evidence in his fight to end the slave trade, and Newton would encourage and support his friend in that effort. Historical accounts seem to imply that John Newton also led William Wilberforce to saving faith in Jesus Christ.[133]

John Newton's profession of slave trading was endorsed by the church, supported by the state, and paid for by virtually every public industry. Yet in his newfound Christianity, he attempted to hold Sunday worship services on board his ship. How ironic. It is little wonder that he began struggling even more with the growing sense inside him that this occupation was wrong, no matter what the clergy, the Parliament, and the public said.

The next command he was given was a slave-trading ship

called the *African*. That voyage was a disaster; there were numerous insurrections among the slaves, and many of them died or committed suicide. A number of his own crew deserted, and several others had to be kept in chains. At one point he thought he would die from yet another illness with high fever.

He wrote, "I just want to live . . . and since my former wretched apostasy was known to hundreds, I want to live to show at least as many of them how I have been changed for God's glory."[134]

He survived that voyage and a year later made another voyage in the interests of the slave trade. By now he was praying that God would give him another calling.

When Newton was about to embark on yet another voyage from Liverpool, England, he suddenly, unexpectedly, inexplicably, suffered an epileptic seizure. It hadn't happened before, and it would never happen again. But his doctor advised him not to sail again.

That was all he needed. He considered it an act of God's hand and immediately resigned his commission. John Newton was finished; he never set sail again.

Sermons and Songs

But now what? He was just twenty-nine years old.

He took a job as tide surveyor (customs inspector), and the following year he was invited to hear a man named George Whitefield preach. Whitefield was preaching nearby—outdoors because no church would allow him to preach indoors—at 5:00 a.m. Four thousand people showed up![135]

Newton was profoundly affected and returned to hear Whitfield again that afternoon. He was able to speak personally with Whitefield, and the two began a friendship that would last their lifetimes.

Along with his study of the Scriptures, John began studying the teachings of Whitefield and others and teaching himself Greek and Hebrew. For the next ten years, he worked at his job and studied the Bible.

Finally, he was ordained and began forty years of pastoral ministry. His first pastorate was in a village named Olney. During his ministry there, the church grew to some two thousand people, requiring that a balcony be added to the building.

Three years into his ministry, a poet named William Cowper, who struggled off and on with depression, moved to Olney and joined his church. Together Newton and Cowper began a Thursday evening prayer service and agreed to take turns writing a hymn for each weekly prayer meeting, which they would teach the congregation. William Cowper's best-known hymn would be, "There is a Fountain Filled with Blood."

Newton and Cowper eventually published a hymnal of all their original hymns.

One of the hymns Newton included was based on 1 Chronicles 17. In that chapter, there are three movements:

First, we see King David's desire to build a permanent temple for the glory of God.

As the chapter progresses, Nathan informs David that he cannot build the temple but that God has promised that David's son Solomon will be able to build it.

The final movement of the chapter is David's praising God for His grace to him, his family, and the nation of Israel.

In verses 16-18, the Bible reads:

Then David the king went in and sat before the Lord and said, "Who am I, O Lord God, and what is my house that You have brought me this far? This was a small thing in

Your eyes, O God; but You have spoken of Your servant's house for a great while to come, and have regarded me according to the standard of a man of high degree, O Lord God. What more can David still say to You concerning the honor bestowed on Your servant?"

In other words, David is saying, "Lord, You know the kind of man I am, and You know the kind of people we are, yet in Your grace, You have done amazing things for us all."

When the hymnal was published, this hymn was printed under the heading, "Faith's Review and Expectation." There were six stanzas originally. The first three were presented as faith's review; the last three as the expectations of faith. We know the hymn by another name:

> Amazing grace! how sweet the sound
> That saved a wretch like me
> I once was lost, but now am found,
> Was blind, but now I see.
>
> 'Twas grace that taught my heart to fear
> And grace my fears relieved,
> How precious did that grace appear,
> The hour I first believed!
>
> Through many dangers, toils and snares,
> I have already come;
> 'Tis grace has brought me safe thus far,
> And grace will lead me home.
>
> The Lord has promised good to me,
> His word my hope secures;
> He will my shield and portion be,
> As long as life endures.

> Yes, when this flesh and heart shall fail,
> And mortal life shall cease;
> I shall possess, within the veil,
> A life of joy and peace.
>
> The earth shall soon dissolve like snow,
> The sun forbear to shine;
> But God who called me here below,
> Will be forever mine.

Eventually, John Newton was called to another church in London, where he served more than twenty years.

One December, Newton received a note from a twenty-six-year-old Member of Parliament asking for an opportunity to have "some serious conversation, but it must be in secret."[136]

The note was from William Wilberforce. He was struggling with a lack of connection with God and had only recently begun reading the Bible for himself. Newton witnessed to Wilberforce and gave him the gospel of grace that only looking to Christ alone would bring salvation.

Wilberforce would later write in his journal, "I called upon old Newton—I was much affected in conversing with him . . . and I have come away looking up to God."[137]

A friendship began between an old, former slave trader and a young reformer who would eventually help bring the slave trade to an end.

Close to his death at eighty-two years of age, when he was completely blind and unable to read his text, friends suggested to John Newton it was time to give up preaching. He responded, "I cannot stop. What! shall the old African Blasphemer stop while he can speak?"[138]

Just weeks before his death, he summed up his life by saying, "My memory is nearly gone. But I remember two things: that I am a great sinner, and that Christ is a great Saviour."[139]

After he died, the words he had dictated for his tombstone were carved, just as he'd ordered:

> John Newton, Clerk,
> Once an infidel and libertine,
> A servant of slaves in Africa,
> Was by the rich mercy of our Lord and Saviour
> Jesus Christ,
> Preserved, restored, pardoned,
> And appointed to preach the faith
> He had long labored to destroy.[140]

CHARLES SPURGEON

Charles Spurgeon entered the world on June 19, 1834, as the son and grandson of pastors. In the years to come, he would become the most profoundly influential, internationally known pastor in the world.

Because of economic necessity, Charles was sent to live with his grandparents when he was two years of age. When he returned to his parents' home at the age of six to begin formal schooling, he was already able to read, having been taught to read the Bible by his godly grandparents.

When Spurgeon returned home, his father also exerted a godly influence over him. But he spoke more of his mother's influence. Evidently, she would gather the children on Sunday evening around the table for Scripture reading and prayer. Spurgeon said she would pray like this: "Now Lord, if my children go on in their sins, it will not be from ignorance that they perish, and my soul must bear witness against them at the day of judgment if they lay not hold of Christ."[141]

Conversion

Even though Spurgeon had a godly heritage, he resisted the work of God's Spirit. He wrote:

> *I must confess that I never would have been saved if I could have helped it. As long as ever I could, I rebelled, and revolted, and struggled against God. When He would have me pray, I would not pray . . . And when I heard, and the tear rolled down my cheek, I wiped it away and defied Him to melt my soul. But long before I began with Christ, He*

began with me.[142]

Spurgeon once said that by the age of sixteen, the Holy Spirit had been plowing his soul with ten horses in his team—the Ten Commandments—and cross plowing it with the gospel.

One Sunday morning the snow was falling so heavy that Charles couldn't get to his own church, so he wandered into a Primitive Methodist chapel. When he arrived a bit late, he discovered that the pastor wasn't even there. In fact, no one knew where the pastor was, so after some awkward delays, another man stood to preach. He was uneducated and to this day unnamed.

The man could barely read, yet he preached on the text, "Look unto me, and be ye saved." He stuck to his text, for he had little else to say. Spurgeon recalled the man's words:

> *"My dear friends," said he, "this is a simple text. It says, Look. Now lookin' don't take a deal of pains. It ain't liftin' your foot or your finger. It is just, 'Look.' Well, a man needn't go to college to learn to look. You may be the biggest fool and yet you can look. You needn't be worth a thousand a year to be able to look. Anyone can look; even a child can look. But then the text says, 'Look unto Me.' . . . Many of ye are lookin' to yourselves, but it's no use lookin' there. You'll never find any comfort in yourselves . . . Look to Christ. The text says, 'Look unto Me.'"[143]*

Spurgeon said that after about ten minutes of such preaching, this layman had quite exhausted what he had to say. But then he noticed young Spurgeon sitting in the back under the balcony. Not recognizing him, but noticing his downcast expression, he focused on Spurgeon and cried out, "Young man, you look miserable. . . . And you will always be miserable—

miserable in life, and miserable in death—if you do not obey my text. But if you obey now, this moment, you will be saved. Young man, look to Jesus! Look! Look! Look!"[144]

And with that, the sermon was over. But God's invitation from His Word delivered in that simple message penetrated Spurgeon's heart, and that day he looked to Christ alone and was indeed saved. His life was changed forever.

The verse Spurgeon heard preached that day is from Isaiah 45, a rich text in which God is speaking through His prophet. The Lord offers an invitation to Israel and anyone else who will listen:

> *Gather yourselves and come; draw near together, you fugitives of the nations; they have no knowledge, who carry about their wooden idol and pray to a god who cannot save. Declare and set forth your case; indeed, let them consult together. Who has announced this from of old? Who has long since declared it? Is it not I, the Lord? And there is no other God besides Me, a righteous God and a Savior; there is none except Me. (verses 20-21)*

Then follows the verse the man proclaimed to Spurgeon (in the King James version from which he was preaching): "Look unto me, and be ye saved, all the ends of the earth; for I am God, and there is none else" (verse 22).

That verse would not only be used by God to call Spurgeon to faith, but it would also become the lifelong passion of Charles Haddon Spurgeon to point everyone in his world to his God and Savior, Jesus Christ.

Ministry Beginnings

Within a year, Charles was invited to preach at the age of

seventeen to a handful of villagers who met in what was formerly a barn. He agreed. And within two years that group of villagers had grown to four hundred people.

Although Spurgeon lacked any formal education, he clearly had an amazing mind and was a voracious reader—devouring half a dozen books a week and accumulating a library of more than 12,000 volumes. And he loved to preach.

At the age of nineteen, he was invited to preach in London at the well-known but dying New Park Street Chapel. It had an auditorium that seated more than 1,200 people and a long history of pastors who were brilliant and biblical. The church had been enveloped by the growing city of London, but it had no outreach to the changing population and no pastor/teacher delivering the truth of God's Word.

Spurgeon initially thought the church's invitation was a mistake, and he even attempted to decline. Why would an uneducated country boy be wanted in the city? But this once vibrant church had heard about this uneducated country boy who spoke with passion and color and truth, and they kept inviting him.

Eventually Charles accepted the invitation and arrived to preach. When he spoke that Sunday, less than two hundred people were present.

History records that his clothing didn't fit him, his hair didn't lay down obediently, and he simply didn't fit the London city scene. His father had already told him he was making a mistake to go, and it appeared he was probably right.

A teenage girl in the congregation that Sunday recalled how Spurgeon's appearance was terribly odd and distracting—if not comical. In her diary Susannah wrote about his poorly trimmed hair, oversized satin coat and blue handkerchief with white spots. She said that he awakened in her "feelings of amusement."[145] He awakened more than that apparently, because within two years she would marry him.

Life and Ministry in London

Before he turned twenty, Charles accepted the call to become pastor at New Park Street Chapel. The church began to explode with growth. Within one year the congregation had outgrown the auditorium, and the people decided to build a new one.

While that church building was under construction, the congregation rented a hall to meet in. This was considered scandalous because churches weren't supposed to meet in public buildings—it was unheard of. But Spurgeon didn't care. After all, he had spent three years preaching in a barn!

A year later the congregation moved into their new church building, which was immediately filled to capacity. So, once again, they rented facilities while another church building was constructed.

By now, Charles Spurgeon was a household name. His dramatic style of preaching with hand gestures and tonal inflections—both of which were quite unusual in this day—as well as word pictures, stories, and humor, created an incredible buzz around London.

His humor especially was cause for concern to many since humor in the pulpit was considered extremely out of line in those days. On one occasion a wealthy woman came up to him and informed him that he was using far too much humor in the pulpit. Spurgeon responded, "Madam, you have no idea how much I'm holding back."

Spurgeon did not find anything spiritual about gloom and despair. After all, Jesus did not say, "Blessed are the gloomy." Spurgeon remarked once that some preachers appear to "have their neckties twisted around their souls."[146]

Pastors all around London were divided in their opinions of young Spurgeon. Some called him a glory hound; others called him the Boy Actor. No matter . . . just about everybody wanted to hear him preach.

Spurgeon's theology was entirely biblically driven. He had already upset his family legacy by becoming a Baptist and refusing to sprinkle infants as his father and grandfather had done for decades. Concerning baptism, he wrote, "Although I love and revere them [his father and grandfather], there is no reason why I should imitate them."[147]

And he wasn't about to mince words or back away from what he earlier called "difficult doctrines." He preached and held high the sovereignty of God, the election of the saints, and a final judgment.

He preferred to think of himself as a mere Christian, declaring, "I am never ashamed to avow myself a Calvinist; I do not hesitate to take the name of Baptist, but if I am asked what is my creed, I reply, 'It is [simply] Jesus Christ.'"[148]

In March 1861 the church moved into their newly built Metropolitan Tabernacle in London. It seated 5,600 people but did not include a pipe organ or any other instrument, because Charles believed anything but the voice was a distraction.

Of course, as Susannah learned during their courtship, the voice too could be a distraction for her soon-to-be husband. Their early premarital days often found Spurgeon correcting sermon manuscripts while Susannah sat, as she would later write, "learning how to be quiet."[149]

Once after they were engaged, Spurgeon completely forgot she was with him and left her behind at a church function. She rushed home to her mother in tears.[150]

All in all, they had a wonderful marriage. Susannah bore twin sons who grew up to love Christ and His church. After Charles's death, his son Thomas took his place as the pastor of the church and Charles Jr. took charge of the orphanage their father had founded.

By the age of thirty-three, Susannah suffered physical difficulties. From a variety of reports, it seems she had a rare cervical operation performed by James Simpson, the father of modern gynecology. But it was to no avail. She became a virtual invalid and for the next twenty-seven years, she seldom heard her husband preach to the thousands of people who packed the sanctuary every week.

In fact, the church grew so much that Spurgeon on one occasion asked all the congregation to *not* come to church the following Sunday so that newcomers who might not be Christians could come and hear the gospel.

On another occasion, he simply asked the congregation to dismiss so that those waiting outside could have their seats. They did, and the building immediately filled up again.

By the end of his ministry, he had seen 14,500 people baptized, and his church had a standing, active membership of 5,300.[151]

In the midst of his ministry in London, Spurgeon had to deal with his own physical issues. He suffered from severe gout, swelling in his joints, rheumatism, and inflammation of the kidneys that brought him intense pain. From the age of thirty-five until he died at fifty-seven, he spent one-third of his time out of the pulpit recovering from his various ailments.

Still he worked eighteen hours a day, enabling him to produce more than 140 books in addition to his pastoral and preaching responsibilities. When his missionary friend David Livingstone asked him, "Charles, how do you manage to do two men's work in a single day?" Spurgeon replied, "You have forgotten there are two of us."[152] He loved the words Paul wrote to the Colossians: "I labor, striving according to His power, which mightily works within me" (Colossians 1:29).

Charles once wrote,

If by excessive labor, we die before reaching the average age of man, worn out in the Master's service, then glory be to God, we shall have so much less of earth and so much more of Heaven. . . . It is our duty and our privilege to exhaust our lives for Jesus. We are not to be living specimens of men in fine preservation, but living sacrifices, whose lot is to be consumed.[153]

That's not exactly the most popular way of thinking these days.

Early in his ministry, Charles founded a school for pastors. He wanted men to get the training he had never received. In this enterprise, his straightforward approach to ministry, along with his blunt humor, became legendary.

On one occasion a search committee wrote to Spurgeon asking for a minister from among his student body. They presented the job description and the salary they would pay. Spurgeon wrote back to them, "The only individual I know who could live on such a salary as you are offering is the angel Gabriel. He wouldn't need cash or clothing; he could just come down from heaven on Sunday and go back up that night; so I advise you to invite Gabriel to be your pastor."[154]

On another occasion, a letter arrived from a pastoral search committee asking if Spurgeon would send them a student who could come and fill their auditorium. Spurgeon replied they didn't have any students that large but that he would send a student who would capably fill the pulpit.

Spurgeon personally interviewed every prospective student. He was looking for what he called the clear evidence of the call of God on their lives. In fact, Spurgeon would turn down so many applicants that he earned the nickname "Parson Slayer."

He simply felt concern for protecting the church from unqualified, ungifted, and even ungodly men.

Of one young man who came to apply for entrance, Spurgeon said that his face looked like "the title-page to a whole volume of pride and conceit." He wrote:

> *He sent word... that he must see me at once. His audacity admitted him; and when he was before me he said, "Sir, I want to enter your College, and should like to enter it at once."... As to his preaching, he could produce the highest testimonials, but hardly thought they would be needed, as a personal interview would convince me of his ability at once. His surprise was great when I said, "Sir, I am obliged to tell you that I cannot receive you." "Why not, Sir?" "I will tell you plainly. You are so dreadfully clever that I could not insult you by receiving you into our College, where we have none but rather ordinary men; the president, tutors, and students, are all men of moderate attainments, and you would have to condescend too much in coming among us."... "Then, Sir, you ought to allow me a trial of my preaching abilities; select me any text you like, or suggest any subject you please, and here in this very room I will preach upon it."*

Spurgeon responded that he felt himself "unworthy of the privilege, so bade him a long farewell."[155]

Spurgeon started more than sixty different ministries, and

the demands upon him were great. Thankfully, he had a photographic memory and remembered everything he had read in books and commentaries and the Scriptures he studied.

On Saturday night he would begin working on his Sunday morning sermon. That's not a good idea unless you have a photographic memory and you've been reading voraciously throughout the week.

Spurgeon was actually a textual preacher. He would expound on one verse or two and wring everything possible from that text. The next Sunday he might be in a different book entirely. Sometimes on Saturday night he just couldn't seem to settle on the text for his sermon, and he would call in desperation to Susannah, whom he affectionately called "Susie" or "Wifey."

"Wifey," he'd say, "come help me." And Susannah took great joy in bringing her Bible into his study and reading to him several passages or texts that had special meaning to her own heart. Suddenly, Spurgeon would seize on one of her verses and say, "That's the one." And within a few hours, he would have a sermon prepared.

The following Monday he would edit the sermon transcript, and it would be sent to newspapers around the world and read by millions of people.

On one particular Saturday night, Spurgeon lay in bed, literally preaching in his sleep. He was clearly asleep yet talking plainly. Susannah got paper and pen and actually took notes; and when Spurgeon awakened, she handed him what he had unconsciously preached that night. He took one look at those notes, immediately discarded the sermon he had prepared, and preached from those notes that Sunday morning.

Another Saturday night, a distinguished religious leader from the community appeared at his door and told the housekeeper that he wanted some time with Mr. Spurgeon. She came and told him about the visitor, and Spurgeon responded that he was busy studying for his sermon and couldn't be interrupted.

The housekeeper went back and gave Spurgeon's answer to the dignified visitor, who became angry and offended. He demanded that she return to Spurgeon's study and announce that he must have misunderstood. He said, "Tell Mr. Spurgeon that the Master's servant is here to see him." Spurgeon sent back his reply: "I am presently occupied with the Master and have no time for His servant."[156]

If you read Spurgeon's works—and I recommend you at least read his devotional entitled *Morning and Evening*—you will discover that above everything Spurgeon was a pastor. He loved people, he loved Christ, and he loved shepherding.

Still, nearly two hundred years later, His writings have the ability to bring wonderful encouragement to discouraged hearts. Consider these words, for example:

> *O dear friend, when thy grief presses thee to the dust, worship there. If that spot has come to be thy Gethsemane, then present there thy strong crying and tears unto thy God. Remember David's words, "Ye people, pour out your hearts"—but do not stop there, finish the quotation—"Ye people, pour out your hearts before Him." Turn the vessel upside down; it is a good thing to empty it, for this grief may ferment into something more sour; turn the vessel upside down, and let every drop run out; let it run out before the Lord.[157]*

Spurgeon also wrote of his own sufferings, saying, "The good that I have received from my sorrows, and pains, and griefs, is altogether incalculable . . . Affliction is the best bit of furniture in my house. It is the best book in a minister's library."[158]

Controversies

As we can imagine, Spurgeon's ministry was often clouded with controversy. Most often it was related to doctrine. Once Spurgeon preached a message condemning infant sprinkling, and it caused an incredible uproar throughout London and beyond. Eventually, American newspaper editors began editing his sermons to take out his attacks against slavery.

Spurgeon simply wasn't interested in the majority opinion of the day. He was interested only in what the Bible teaches.

Some of the controversies were of his own making, however.

Charles Spurgeon and Joseph Parker were two of the most famous pastors in the Victorian era in England. Spurgeon preached to some 10,000 in two Sunday services; Parker's congregation was second in size only to Spurgeon's.

Early in their ministries they fellowshipped often and even exchanged pulpits. But, unfortunately, they had a disagreement. Spurgeon accused Joseph Parker of being an unspiritual pastor because he often attended the theater, where plays and operas were performed. Parker fired back, criticizing Spurgeon as a poor example because he smoked cigars, both in private and in public. Each considered the other of being misled and of misleading others by example.

Their words became sharp. Their disagreement was such news that reports of it were carried in the London newspapers. Two great men of the faith broke fellowship with one another, and their friendship would never be the same.[159]

The story is also told that Spurgeon's friend D. L. Moody, America's most famous pastor/evangelist, was visiting Spurgeon and preaching in Spurgeon's pulpit. Moody asked Spurgeon when was he going to give up those awful cigars. And

Spurgeon pointed a finger into Moody's considerable midsection and said, "When you get rid of this."

I use these examples to remind us that great men of faith are not flawless. They can bicker and argue and even divide over issues that are not critical to the gospel of Christ.

Spurgeon's final years were marked by what came to be called the "Downgrade Controversy." He charged pastors in the Baptist Union—a fellowship he belonged to—with neglecting the gospel and dumbing down doctrine. He attacked their growing accommodation of the recently printed theories of Charles Darwin, and he decried any compromise on God's literal, miraculous, six days of creation.

Hundreds of pastors were incensed with his accusations, and he was eventually voted out of the Baptist Union. A few years after being censured by his fellow pastors, he died.

History has vindicated Spurgeon's warnings, and they are still freshly needed today.

Look to Christ

Throughout his ministry and life, Spurgeon never got very far from that verse that arrested his attention and brought salvation to his soul. He had looked to Christ, and acceptance by Christ became his theme throughout his life. It is evident in these words he wrote:

> *How marvelous that we, worms, mortals, sinners, should be the objects of divine love! But it is only "in the Beloved." Some Christians seem to be accepted in their own experience, at least, that is their apprehension. When their spirit is lively, and their hopes bright, they think God accepts them, for they feel so [happy], so heavenly-minded, so drawn above the earth! But when their souls cleave to*

the dust, they are the victims of the fear that they are no longer accepted....

Rejoice then, believer, in this: you are accepted "in the Beloved." You look within, and you say, "There is nothing acceptable here!" But look at Christ, and see if there is not everything acceptable there. Your sins trouble you; but God has cast your sins behind His back and you are accepted in the Righteous One. You have to fight with corruption, and to wrestle with temptation, but you are already accepted in Him who has overcome the powers of evil. The devil tempts you; be of good cheer, he cannot destroy you, for you are accepted in Him.[160]

Look to Christ alone.

GEORGE MUELLER

In her book *Mystery on the Desert*, Maria Reiche described for her readers the unique lines created by the Indians on a desert floor in Peru centuries ago. Shallow trenches circled around and then suddenly stopped. Short mounds seemed to randomly appear without any sense or pattern.

For centuries, these twisting, turning lines and mounds and depressions were a mystery. Some thought they were mystical patterns for some sort of worship system. Others thought they were ancient remnants of an irrigation system.

In 1939, the mystery was solved when Paul Kosok, a professor of anthropology, got into an airplane and flew overhead. As he looked down, he discovered that one of the patterns clearly formed the outline of a bird. Other images soon came into view. These seemingly random lines were designed as landscape drawings of an array of birds and other animals.[161]

Once he flew high overhead, Kosok gained the perspective he needed to see clearly what the lines really were. Imagine creating artistic forms of beauty you can fully appreciate and understand only from a higher perspective. Isn't that a wonderful analogy of the Christian life?

A Higher Perspective

In Paul's letter to the Romans, he makes a rather bold statement in chapter 8. In fact, it's so bold and dramatic that many Christians have memorized it:

> *And we know that God causes all things to work together for good to those who love God, to those who are called ac-*

cording to His purpose. (Romans 8:28)

Paul is basically saying that all those seemingly random patterns of your life that seem somewhat mysterious and at times meandering—starting and stopping, fluctuating up and then quickly down—demand a higher-than-earth perspective.

The apostle is giving us that higher view on life. And in doing so, he speaks with confidence, saying, "We *know*."

We should notice too that Paul did not say, "We know that all things *are* good," because they aren't; some of those valleys are deep, and some of those hills are treacherous. Rather, he said that we can be confident of this: "God causes all things to work together for good."

The Greek verb translated "work together" is *sunergeō*, from which we get our English word *synergism*. Synergism is the combined action of two or more things that have a greater total effect than the sum of their individual effects.[162]

That's exactly what Paul has in mind. Any one event in your life may not seem to work out. But Paul is saying that *all* events synergistically produce something far better than the combined *individual* events could.

And he tells us that "God causes *all things* to work together for good." Does the "all things" include even evil and sin, false accusations, injustice, betrayal, broken relationships, cruelty, pain and suffering, hatred, jealousy, abandonment, and murder?

Yes. In fact, Jesus Christ experienced all those things over the last few hours of His earthly life, and God caused all those single events to work together to produce something good.

Paul concludes by saying God produces this good for "those who love God . . . those who are called according to His purpose." These phrases are simply two descriptions of Christians.

As a Christian, you love God and you've been called by God to a purpose that He will ultimately fulfill in your life—not only *now* but also eventually in your glorification and perfection in Christ Jesus. Every random hill, every twisting valley, every sudden stop, every sharp turn, every climb up, and every step down is the artistry of God at work.

There's a lesser known Old Testament verse that could be called the twin verse of Romans 8:28. It's Psalm 84:11:

For the Lord God is a sun and shield; the Lord gives grace and glory; no good thing does He withhold from those who walk uprightly.

Again, this is a reference to all believers, and with incredible confidence, the sons of Korah composed this statement, declaring that God withholds "no good thing" from His children.

So, if you don't have something, it's because God didn't consider it good for you—at least not up to this time. And if you have it, it's because God considered it good for His ultimate purposes in your life!

This concept and these texts of Scripture form the foundation for one of the most amazing testimonies of faith in modern history.

In fact, one particular man literally staked his life and ministry on the bold confidence that God will never withhold what is ultimately good for His beloved and that all events work synergistically together for ultimate good.

An Unlikely Choice

Before we get to this man's lifelong perspective and fruitful ministry, we should note how unlikely a candidate for God's service he was.

His name was George Mueller. He was born in the kingdom of Prussia (now Germany) in 1805, and his native language was German.

It seems both his parents were unbelievers. His father was a tax collector for the government. He made plenty of money and seemed to live for it. George and his brother routinely stole money from their father in order to support their own lives of gambling, drinking, and immorality.

His father decided to make a Lutheran minister out of George, not because of spiritual interests, but because Lutheran ministers were supported by the state and had a comfortable life.

George was fourteen when his mother died, but for some time he was unaware that she had even died because, he wrote, "I . . . was playing cards until two in the morning, and on the next day, being the Lord's day, I went with some of my companions in sin to a tavern, and then, being filled with strong beer, we went about the streets half intoxicated."[163]

At age sixteen, George Mueller found himself in jail, charged with stealing. Upon his release, his father beat him. He straightened up a bit, learned his undergraduate subjects, and a few years later began seminary studies, though he was still unconverted.

George later estimated that of the 900 divinity students at his seminary, only 9 of them were Christians. The graduates would all go on to make their living from government funds, renting pews in the church, and performing liturgical services, weddings, and funerals.

While in seminary, Mueller was invited to an evangelical prayer meeting with a handful of humble believers. He was struck by their simple singing of hymns and the sermon that was read—and it was read because it was illegal for someone to preach and expound on Scripture without an ordained minister present. And, sadly, most of the ordained clergymen were unbelievers.

But what struck Mueller the most was how the meeting began—with everyone in the room getting down on their knees and praying. He said, "I had *never* either seen any one on his knees, nor had I myself prayed on my knees." He wrote that that evening on his bed, "[God] began a work of grace in me . . . that evening was the turning point in my life."[164]

He was twenty years of age when he gave his life to Jesus Christ as Lord and Savior. Four years later he arrived in England as a missionary to the Jews. It was a ministry inhibited by his limited ability to speak English and a ministry he soon would leave.

A year later, he was baptized by immersion, convinced that Scripture allowed for this mode alone. He also became pastor of a church in Devonshire, England, where he met and married Mary Groves.

Walking by Faith

Following his marriage, George quickly gave up a formal pastoral salary, determined to receive from people only what they joyfully gave for his allowance. He also stopped the practice of renting out pews, arguing that this step of faith was necessary since the church was guilty of committing the same sin the apostle James warned of in James 2—giving the best seats to the rich and asking the poor to stand by the wall.

While he was pastoring in Devonshire, Mary gave birth to a stillborn child. A year later, in 1832, and at the age of twenty-seven, George became pastor of a small church in Bristol, England. He would remain pastor there for some fifty years.

At Bristol they had a daughter born to them, and they

named her Lydia. Later they had another child, a son who lived for only three months. A few years later, they had another stillborn son.

In the meantime, George and his wife decided to take as many orphans off the streets as they could feed. They renovated their home so they could house thirty girls. It wasn't long before the neighbors complained about the noise and the regular disruption of public utilities. Evidently, the needs of all those girls didn't leave much water for the rest of the neighborhood.

This was the beginning of a ministry George Mueller and his wife would see God use in a tremendously fruitful manner in the years to come. Within ten years, and without any appeal for funds, a house was built to accommodate up to three hundred children.

While George Mueller was a pastor for more than fifty years, he is known primarily for his orphanages. Those orphanages eventually included five buildings caring for 2,050 orphans at any one time. Yet there are two surprising aspects of this ministry that are not so well known.

First, Mueller's orphanages were only a part of his ministry vision.

He founded the Scripture Knowledge Institute, which had a fivefold commitment:

- To assist the education of children and adults by providing biblical curriculum
- To distribute Bibles
- To distribute biblical materials, tracts, and literature
- To support missionaries
- To board, clothe, and scripturally educate destitute children who have lost both parents by death[165]

In nineteenth-century England, a supposedly civilized culture, the conditions for destitute children, and especially orphans, were appalling. When George Mueller began his ministry to orphans in 1834, there were over 7,000 children under the age of eight who were in prison![166] His commitment to ministering to orphans was very much needed and very significant, but it was still just one part of his larger ministry of teaching and evangelizing.

The second surprising element of his orphanage ministry was one of his primary reasons for establishing this work.

Mueller was fully convinced that God would not withhold from him any good thing, and he saw the orphan ministry as a means of demonstrating to other believers that God is trustworthy and would not withhold from them any good thing either.

So, along with addressing the spiritual and temporal needs of orphans, a primary reason for establishing the orphan house was "that God may be glorified, should He be pleased to furnish . . . the means, [to show] that it is not a vain thing to trust in Him; and that thus the faith of His children may be strengthened."[167]

Because of this mission and perspective, George made it his practice to never directly appeal for funds but simply to report how God provided. So, he published a report annually. It included personal testimonies and the stories of God's wonderful provision though the faithful support of so many friends.

In his seventies, he wrote, "We doubt not that the Lord has again and again used [these reports] as instruments in leading persons to help us with their means."[168] In other words, he simply told the story of God's faithfulness, and God moved people to respond and provide all that George and his family and his ministries needed.

But there were times, especially in the early years, when the finances didn't come in until just in time. A close friend of Mueller's reported that on one occasion he stood at breakfast with the orphans, their plates in front of them and nothing on the table. He stood and gave thanks for their breakfast. Immediately, there was a knock at the door. A baker entered, saying he had been up all night, unable to sleep, baking fresh bread for everyone.

And just then came another knock. A village milkman whose cart had broken down right in front of the orphanage entered to say that he would like to give the milk to the children so he could empty and fix his wagon. The milk was enough for all.[169]

Years later George Mueller wrote these words:

It needed to be something which could be seen, even by the natural eye. Now, if I, a poor man, simply by prayer and faith, obtained, without asking any individual, the means for establishing and carrying on an Orphan-House: there would be something which, with the Lord's blessing, might be instrumental in strengthening the faith of the children of God besides being a testimony to the consciences of the unconverted, of the reality of the things of God.[170]

Imagine this life mission—to have the opportunity to become a visual aid to the world of God's faithfulness. George Mueller just wanted an opportunity to demonstrate that God is real and faithful and will not withhold anything He considers good from those who walk with Him.

The ministry Mueller started would continue long after his death under the leadership of his son-in-law. At the end of Mueller's life, however, the Scripture Knowledge Institute had accomplished the following:

- Distributed 244,000 biblical resources
- Distributed 285,000 entire Bibles and 1.4 million New Testaments
- Supported numerous missionaries, including Hudson Taylor
- Cared for and educated just over 10,000 orphans.

What can't be fully calculated is the effect of his ministry on others. One author said that his ministry so inspired others, that at least one hundred thousand orphans were cared for in England alone.[171]

To study the life of George Mueller is to study the life of someone who simply took God at His word. His simple reading of the Bible—some two hundred times throughout his ministry—and his simple prayer life continue to be commendable examples.

When each child in the orphanage became old enough to live on his own, George would personally pray with him and put a Bible in his right hand and a coin in his left. He would explain to the young person that if he held onto what was in his right hand, God would make sure there was always something in his left hand as well. That's how he himself lived.

When George gave his life to Christ, he was struck by believers getting on their knees to pray. And that became his practice as well.

When George Mueller was ninety-two years old, he led a prayer meeting at his church on Wednesday evening. He had asked that the next morning his hosts bring him a cup of tea, but when they knocked on the door the following morning at 7:00 a.m., there was no answer. They entered and found him beside his bed, having died while praying on his knees.

That's how he lived—and that's how he died.

Today George Mueller remains a living testimony to us all that God does not withhold any good thing from His children. The steep hills and deep valleys and sudden stops may not always seem so good, but God is creating divine art, and with a higher perspective—now and certainly later—we'll see that God was indeed providing everything necessary for all those who know Him and follow Him.

WILLIAM COWPER

William Cowper's life was changed by these words of the apostle Paul:

Being justified as a gift by His grace through the redemption which is in Christ Jesus; whom God displayed publicly as a propitiation in His blood through faith. (Romans 3:24-25a)

When we think of the death and atoning sacrifice of Christ, there are a number of words that might come to our minds—words like *sacrifice, offering, atonement, substitution*, and *redemption*. The first word that pops into our minds is probably not *propitiation*. And that's likely because we have a hard time pronouncing it, much less understanding it.

However, there is a volume of theological truth wrapped up in this one word, *propitiation*. Wayne Grudem's *Systematic Theology* defines propitiation as "a sacrifice that bears God's wrath to the end and in so doing changes God's wrath toward us into favor."[172] The reason *propitiation* is not one of the most exciting and encouraging words to people today is because we have forgotten the truth that mankind is in deep trouble and facing the eternal wrath of God.

There is a myth that is growing in popularity today. It's the idea that the God of the Old Testament was angry and judgmental and vindictive, but the God of the New Testament is all about love and mercy and grace. The only reason people would buy this is because they have never really read either the Old or the New Testament. Consider just the following examples where the New Testament speaks of God's wrath and judgment:

- In the book of Romans, Paul introduces us to God as One who is revealing His wrath from heaven (Romans 1:18).
- The writer of Hebrews describes God as "a consuming fire" (Hebrews 12:29).
- Paul says when God the Son returns to earth in the future, He "will be revealed from heaven with His mighty angels in flaming fire, dealing out retribution to those who do not know God" (2 Thessalonians 1:7-8).
- And the apostle Peter describes the future judgment on Planet Earth in these words: "By His word the present heavens and earth are being reserved for fire, kept for the day of judgment and destruction of ungodly men" (2 Peter 3:7).
- Jude describes salvation from eternal judgment as being snatched out of the fire (Jude 1:23).

Mankind doesn't like the idea of God being filled with righteous anger and wrath against sinners. Yet the truth is that apart from Christ, we stand under the wrath and impending judgment of God (John 3:36). The gospel of Christ is the free offer of being rescued from God's just judgment. This is the glory and relief and joy of the gospel. God sent His Son to be our propitiation, our substitute who would endure the wrath of the holy God and satisfy the demands of His justice.

I remember as a kid reading about a fire that swept across the prairie, devastating crops and houses and anything else that stood in its path. One farmer saw the smoke when the fire was still a long way off, but he knew there was no way to stop the fire and he and his family would never be able to outrun it. There was nowhere to run and nowhere to hide. Then he did something odd; he ran and got some coals from the fireplace and lit his own field on fire. He knew the wind would sweep the fire along a mile or so ahead of the rapidly approaching prairie fire. He then packed up his family in their wagon and drove it onto that smoldering field he had just burned to the ground. There they camped in the middle of that field and waited. Within moments that great wall of fire came toward them and right up to the edge of their field. Finding nothing to feed its hunger because the field was already burned, the fire licked its way around the edges of the field and eventually moved away.

They were safe. Why? Because they were standing on ground that had already been burned. That ground they were standing on was their *propitiation*. It had already satisfied the fire. It had already endured the demands of that prairie fire and could not be burned again.

If by faith you stand in Christ, you will never have to face the fiery judgment of God because you are standing on that which has already satisfied the wrath of God. God's wrath has already burned against His Son, and you will never experience it. You are safe in Christ forever.

Propitiation in the Life of William Cowper

Never was this great truth of propitiation through the offering of Christ more desperately needed than in the heart and mind of one of England's greatest poets, William Cowper. Cowper (pronounced like Cooper) was born in England in 1731 and died just before his seventieth birthday. His father was a pastor, though more than likely unconverted. Cowper could remember as a child seeing people leave their homes at four o'clock in the morning to go hear George Whitefield preach in some open field.[173]

Cowper's mother was devoted to him, but his childhood was marked by sadness. He experienced the deaths of five siblings and eventually the death of his beloved mother when he was only six years of age. He never forgot the deep sorrow he experienced as a little boy. Unfortunately, his father gave him no sympathy. And two household servant girls used his sorrow to manipulate him, promising him that if he acted perfectly, his mother would come back home. She never did, and Cowper never got over losing her.

Being sent off to boarding school was another horrific experience for this sensitive, artistic boy. There he was bullied mercilessly and often beaten by the other students. Eventually, he pursued a legal career by the arrangement of his father, but he did so without much seriousness and consequently without much success.

At the age of twenty-one, William sank into his first paralyzing depression. It would be the first of four major battles with mental breakdowns so severe he did nothing more than sit and stare out a window.[174]

At times he suffered terrible nightmares, heard voices, and experienced hallucinations. But in the 1700s there was little understanding of—and even less medical treatment for—depression and mental disorders.

The poetry of a believer from a century and a half earlier gave hope to his heart and helped him recover from this first deep depression, but he still knew nothing of the gospel. Eleven years later Cowper suffered another complete breakdown. This time, in God's providence, he was placed in the insane asylum at St. Albans. Although the villagers called it the "Madhouse," for Cowper, now thirty-three years old, it became a refuge.

The asylum's director was fifty-eight-year-old Dr. Nathaniel Cotton, a committed evangelical who loved the gospel and wanted all his patients to hear it. Dr. Cotton, who engaged Cowper in lengthy conversations, had the habit of leaving Bibles throughout the hospital, where patients would find them opened to certain passages. One morning, by the grace of God, William Cowper sat on a window bench waiting for breakfast to be served. Fluttering in the breeze next to him was an open

Bible. He picked it up and the first verse he saw was Romans 3:25: "Whom God displayed publicly as a propitiation in His blood through faith."

He would later write, "I saw the sufficiency of the atonement he had made, my pardon sealed in his blood, and all the fullness and completeness of his justification. In a moment I believed, and received the Gospel.... Unless the Almighty arm had not been under me, I think I should have died with gratitude and joy. My eyes filled with tears, and my voice choked with transport. I could only look up to heaven in silent fear, overwhelmed with love and wonder."[175] Several months later, William Cowper was released from the "Madhouse" at St. Albans.

But his mental and emotional battles were not over. Undoubtedly a contributing factor was an earlier romance with his cousin Theodora, whom he courted for several years. The two became engaged to be married, but her father refused to give her hand in marriage to William. While Theodora's father cited the inappropriateness of cousins marrying, he seemed to have deeper reasons for his objection to the marriage. Though they separated and Theodora moved away, she maintained her love for William throughout the rest of her life. She never married and quietly followed William's growing fame as a poet, along with his battles with depression. At one point in his life when he was in financial need, she supported him with gifts passed through a mutual friend. He never found out the gifts were from her. After their breakup, William never saw Theodora again. He addressed some nineteen poems to her, some written years after they parted.[176]

William wrote to a friend that he always seemed to have three threads of despair to only one thread of hope in his mind. In his later years, he was convinced all over again that God did not love him and that he would be the only person to have believed the gospel of Christ yet be rejected by God at the gates of heaven. It was a battle Cowper would wage his entire Christian life. But in the midst of it all, William Cowper wrote poems about the gospel and the grace of God that the church is still singing today.

Principles from the Life of William Cowper

Summarizing Cowper's life and tracing his footprints through tracks of truth reveal five principles worth observing and imitating.

Personal Frailties May Be Unrelenting, but They Do Not Signify the Displeasure or Rejection of God

It is tragic for any church or believer to look down on fellow believers who struggle with mental illness as if they are less loved by God or less diligent in their faith. They may very well be the heroic disciples among us.

The brain is as fallen and weak as our arthritic shoulders and knees that give us pain and for which we get medicine and therapy and assistance. If we are honest, we will all admit to periods of discouragement and even despair. Those who think the mature in faith will never struggle need to go visit Job as he sits on the ash heap, suffering from numerous physical ailments, mourning the death of his children and the loss of his family and financial empire. They need to hear Job telling those men who attempted to counsel him, "It would have been better if I'd been stillborn or my mother had miscarried me. God has abandoned me." Job despaired of life itself. So also did Moses, Elijah, Jeremiah, and Jonah. These men indeed had faith, but they also had moments of despair.

William Cowper despaired of life to the point of taking matters into his own hands. Several times over the course of his life, he attempted suicide, but each time he failed. On one occasion he attempted to drink poison but couldn't get his fingers to open the bottle no matter how hard he tried. On another occasion he tried to hang himself, but just after passing into unconsciousness, the rope broke and he revived.[177]

His instability, despair, and depression were so deep that life seemed to be absent of hope. But God had not forsaken him. In fact, over the years, God would speak through him great truths of grace and providence and mercy.

Personal Friends May Not Eliminate Your Battles, but They Can Share Them

Without medical knowledge or treatment available to him, God brought Cowper to points of sanity and reason largely through the influence and encouragement of close friends.

When he was released from the asylum, Cowper rented space in the home of an older woman and fellow believer. She became to him, for the rest of his life, a caring mother figure to replace the mother he had lost as a child.

By the providence of God, this woman's home in the village of Olney was next door to another poet. That poet was also a pastor—a man who had been a slave trader in his past and still struggled with the shame of what he had done. His name was John Newton, the man who wrote those wonderful words, "Amazing grace how sweet the sound that saved a wretch like me." Newton became Cowper's pastor and close friend.

Newton didn't believe anybody should ever have an idle moment. His answer to discouragement and depression was, in a word, service. So it wasn't long before he had Cowper assisting him in visitation and helping the poor. Newton believed that introspection would accomplish nothing; our hearts and our hands should be busy serving others. That was Newton's practical philosophy for helping his friend.

Newton also encouraged Cowper to keep at his poetry and compose poems the church could recite and later sing. Cowper eventually wrote 68 different poems and added them to Newton's collection of 280. Together they published them in 1779 as *The Olney Hymns.* It became the most influential hymnal in the evangelical church for nearly a century.

Painful Struggles Might Not Eliminate Ministry Opportunities but Rather Enlarge Them

One of the Olney hymns came out of a dark period in Cowper's life, when he again attempted unsuccessfully to take his own life. Realizing that God had once more spared him, he sat down to write. What he wrote would become, and remain to this day, two and a half centuries later, one of the greatest and deepest descriptions of God's sovereignty ever put into poetry. Note some of the stanzas from this great hymn.

> God moves in a mysterious way
> His wonders to perform;
> He plants His footsteps in the sea
> And rides upon the storm.
>
> Deep in unfathomable mines
> Of never failing skill
> He treasures up His bright designs
> And works His sovereign will.
>
> Judge not the Lord by feeble sense,
> But trust Him for His grace;
> Behind a frowning providence
> He hides a smiling face.
>
> Blind unbelief is sure to err
> And scan His work in vain;
> God is His own interpreter,
> And He will make it plain.[178]

Cowper's suffering provided a depth and insight that produced profound expressions of the grace and providence of God. Late in life he wrote a poem entitled, "The Task," which described ordinary life from a believer's point of view. It was widely purchased and became a powerful introduction of the gospel to the common person.

Personal Interaction with Nature Can't Replace God's Word, but It Can Enlighten and Encourage Us

During one of Cowper's periods of recovery, some children in the Olney village brought him three baby rabbits that needed care. He took them in and helped them thrive. Soon he began taking in other animals that needed some form of help. He planted a garden to help feed them. It wasn't long before he was growing melons and cabbages, even writing what he was learning about sowing and planting.[179] Eventually he was looking after a large number of rabbits and guinea pigs, a squirrel, pigeons, two dogs, several cats, two canaries, and two goldfinches, along with hens, ducks, and some geese.

He wasn't just feeding them or tending to them, however; he was observing them. He began drawing analogies between the animals and garden plants and truths about God's care and design. He began recording his observances in his journal. Cowper even made up a fun biography of the three rabbits. He began referring to himself as God's under-gardener in Paradise. He enjoyed working in his little greenhouse, growing cauliflower, broccoli, cucumbers, and pineapples, along with an array of flowers and myrtles and plants.[180] On one occasion he wrote to a friend and revealed that caring for animals and plants and working as a gardener helped him "fight off melancholy and hypochondria."[181]

There is little doubt that although William Cowper suffered four major setbacks in his life, he would have suffered much more without friends, a willingness to serve others, and a growing fascination and participation with some of God's creation.

There is a principle to be applied here, both simple and profound: take your eyes off yourself. Go out and serve others. Relate nature to Scripture. Enjoy the glory of Lord's creative handiwork—study it and observe the analogies you see to the Word of God, the character of God, and the gospel of God.

In practical terms, serve the Lord and serve others in need. Take a walk outdoors, put up a birdfeeder, or plant some flowers. Get a dog. Get your hands dirty by digging and planting and pruning out in your yard.

Powerful Faith Does Not Guarantee Freedom from Suffering, but It Does Provide a Guided Tour through It

Cowper once remarked to a friend that God had marked him out for misery. His friend responded, "That is not your case; you are marked out for mercy."[182] William Cowper struggled with doubt, depression, and even despair, but he was indeed an object of God's mercy. And because of that and because he clung to his faith, we sing still today the wonderful, deep words he wrote about God's gospel of grace and mercy.

His greatest hymn—"There Is a Fountain Filled with Blood"—reflects the despair of being under the wrath of God without propitiation. But it also rings with the gospel hope that God sent Jesus and that He endured the wrath of God for us.

> There is a fountain filled with blood
> Drawn from Immanuel's veins;
> And sinners, plunged beneath that flood,
> Lose all their guilty stains.

And so we can believe by faith this great truth God gave us —the truth that converted William Cowper—that we are "justified as a gift by His grace." We can never measure up; it is a *gift* that comes "through the redemption which is in Christ Jesus; whom God displayed publicly as a propitiation in His blood through faith."

This stanza sums up the thought:

> The dying thief rejoiced to see
> That fountain in his day;
> And there may I, though vile as he,
> Wash all my sins away.

Here we see the despair and the deliverance. God's wrath is turned to God's favor.

At the age of sixty-nine, William Cowper died in his sleep. One of his friends who saw him just after he died remarked that William had an expression on his face that could only be described with the word *surprise*. What did it mean? Was he surprised that he indeed was being escorted into the courts of heaven, a place he thought he would be rejected from? Surprised that God was in fact satisfied with him because he was in Christ? Surprised perhaps that he was doing what he had spoken of doing in this hymn the church has been singing now for nearly three hundred years? Here's what he dared to write even as he struggled with his own doubts:

> When this poor lisping, stammering tongue
> Lies silent in the grave.
> Then in a nobler, sweeter song,
> I'll sing Thy power to save.

William Cowper is still singing of Christ's power to save. And we who through faith have found satisfaction in Christ, the One who has satisfied the wrath of God, will one day stand before the Lord with Cowper and a multitude of others and sing this great truth now fulfilled in all our lives. No matter our frailties, disabilities, failures, or doubts, we who cling to Christ will one day—even as now—sing of His power to save.

KATHARINA LUTHER

It was late on Easter Sunday, April 5, 1523. A brave merchant and his nephew drove a wagon filled with empty fish barrels into a convent, where nuns were fast asleep. Not all of them were sleeping, however. A dozen women heard the signal and raced down the stone hallway of their sleeping quarters to hide inside the barrels.

Once inside, the nuns made their daring getaway. A day later, they arrived at the doorstep of a monastery and were greeted by a former monk who had helped plan their escape.

Escaping the Convent

One of these nuns was twenty-four-year-old Katharina von Bora. Years earlier, Katharina had been taken to a convent following the death of her mother. At the tender age of five, her father paid the lowest fee allowable for entrance, and she was raised as a nun. At the age of sixteen, she was "married to Christ" and officially became a nun.[183] Apparently, she never corresponded with her father again.

Katharina took her vows of obedience, chastity, and poverty seriously. She joined with other nuns in their efforts to deny the comforts of the flesh. Food and sleep were kept to a minimum, as nuns were taught to consider self-deprivation a pathway to holiness.

Katharina's day began at 2:00 a.m., as she rose with the other nuns for prayer. Then, at 4:00 a.m., she rose again for prayer. Throughout the day, at 7:00 a.m., 9:00 a.m., 12:00 p.m.,

3:00 p.m., 5:00 p.m., and 7:00 p.m., she would set aside her chores for more prayers and hymns and Scripture readings.[184]

Talking was considered a distraction from holy service, and friendships were nearly impossible to develop. Abstaining from particular foods like meat was also believed to suppress fleshly desires and contribute to holiness and God's approval.[185] This was the lifestyle to which Katharina devoted herself. In fact, the official records of the convent reveal that there was not a single complaint or reprimand ever registered against Katharina von Bora.

But during those years, news from the outside world reached those cloistered hallways, and sermons were smuggled into the convent by delivery boys. The news was dramatic and revolutionary: Martin Luther had dared defy church tradition! The German priest and theology professor was preaching that salvation is a gift from God to anyone who believes. He was preaching that monasteries and convents were not a guaranteed pathway to heaven after all and that forgiveness is not by penance, ritual, baptism, sacrament, and self-sacrifice. Rather, he was teaching that the path to God is by faith alone in the sacrifice of Jesus Christ alone.

We don't know all the details of what Katharina heard inside that convent or the doubts she struggled with as she attempted to find holiness and acceptance before God. We *do* know from a few of her own words preserved for us in history that she "prayed feverishly and diligently" in the convent.[186] We also know that one of her diligent prayer requests related specifically to that Easter Sunday night when she risked everything from her past and everything in her future—if not heaven itself—by believing the Reformation teaching of Luther and others and acting upon it.

At twenty-four years of age, she climbed inside that fish barrel in the middle of the night and made her escape. Within twenty-four hours, she would meet the primary preacher of this radical reformation movement: Martin Luther.

Marrying the Reformer

Like Katharina, Martin knew little of family love growing up. When Martin was caught in a sudden storm and feared for his life, he promised the patron Saint Ann that if he survived he would enter the monastery and become a monk. But when he told his father of his decision, his father was livid.

He followed through on his promise, however, and like Katharina, he became one of the most dedicated members of the monastery. In fact, he nearly drove his religious mentors crazy with his lengthy confessions. One day, in an effort to rid his conscience of guilt, he confessed his sins for nearly six hours, until his confessor became too exhausted to hear anymore.

After seven years of monastic life, Luther's mentor, Johann von Staupitz, put an end to the torment and ordered him to leave the monastery and begin teaching at the University of Wittenberg.[187] He moved into a monastery near the university called the Black Cloister, so called because of the dark clothing worn by the resident Augustinian monks.

In Wittenberg, Luther began to teach through the books of Romans and Galatians. Over the course of his studies, Paul's words in Romans 1 deeply impacted Luther and changed his life forever.

> *I am not ashamed of the gospel, for it is the power of God for salvation to everyone who believes, to the Jew first and also to the Greek. For in it the righteousness of God is re-*

vealed from faith to faith; as it is written, "But the righteous [just] man shall live by faith." (Romans 1:16-17)

Luther later wrote, "Although I was an impeccable monk, I stood before God as a sinner troubled in conscience, and I had no confidence that my merit would satisfy God."[188]

Through his study of the Scriptures, Luther came to realize that the righteousness of God (and thus being made right with God) comes not by self-denial or self-sacrifice or individual merit or avoiding meat or getting up early in the morning to pray. It is a gift given freely by God and freely received by faith alone.[189]

Martin Luther was rocked by that discovery. The church wasn't teaching this truth, but the Bible was. Martin risked his life and his future on *sola fide*, faith alone, based on what he called *sola scriptura*, the Scriptures alone. "Luther argued for the authority of Scripture alone over doctrine, papal primacy, and even the Church itself."[190]

Luther wrote, "The whole of Scripture took on a new meaning, and . . . [the righteousness that comes from God] became to me inexpressibly sweet in greater love. This passage of Paul became to me a gate to heaven."[191] It was not the monastery or the church but the Scriptures and the gospel of Christ that most delighted Luther.

Fast-forward a few years, and we find forty-year-old Martin Luther standing at the doorway of the Black Cloister, welcoming a cartful of nuns he had helped to escape from their convent. The nuns would have curtsied and said hello to the most famous preacher in Germany, the resident theology professor at the University of Wittenberg, and the leader of what we now call the Protestant Reformation.

Within a few months, three of the nuns returned to their families, and eight found husbands with the help of Martin the "matchmaker," but there was one nun left without a family or a husband—Katharina von Bora. Luther tried to marry her off to a friend of his who had shown interest in Katherina, but the friend left town. Months later, they learned he had married someone else. The only other eligible bachelor Luther could think of was a pastor who lived nearby. He was intelligent, resourceful, had an earned doctorate in theology, and was faithfully pastoring a church. He seemed to be the perfect husband for Katharina, but there was one problem: she didn't like him.[192] And she let that be known.

Luther was exasperated over the whole thing, as he felt responsible to find suitable situations for all twelve nuns he had helped escape. But two years had passed, and this former nun evidently had a mind of her own. What she did next was shocking. She informed Luther through a mutual friend that he needed to abandon his plan to marry her off to his pastor friend, but, she added, if Luther himself sought her hand, she would not refuse him.[193] She was essentially proposing to Martin Luther!

Interestingly, Luther had challenged the very structure and theology of the church and written clearly that God's design for church leaders was not celibacy but a loving and faithful marriage. He had written widely on the blessing of children and the ideal of God's design through family life. He openly ridiculed the hypocrisy of church leaders who kept mistresses. And he had expounded on the obvious nature of God's created order for a man to find a wife and to faithfully love her.

In spite of all this, however, Luther never planned to marry because of his travels and work and because of the growing threats to his life. He actually believed he would be martyred at any time or die from an illness. Now a twenty-six-year-old runaway nun had just proposed to him.

He was stunned along with everyone else around him. There was absolutely no way in the world he was going to say yes ... and then he did. Like old Boaz to whom young Ruth "proposed," Martin was shocked—and then smitten.

Later, he wrote that he married Katharina to make his father happy, since his father wanted grandchildren. He also wrote that he wed Katharina to rile up the pope, to cause the angels to laugh, and to cause the devil to weep.[194] He stated that he wanted to practice what he had been preaching about marriage and that the home was designed by God to be a living demonstration of Christ and the church.

This was a most unlikely marriage. There was no way it would ever survive. In the sixteenth century, the church didn't have married leaders, and the people didn't have model marriages to imitate.

Setting the Standard of Christian Marriage

Philip Schaff, the historian, wrote that the Luthers' marriage would set the standard for the Christian family for centuries to come.[195] If you think people are watching the marriages of the royal family in England, you can't imagine how the world watched the marriage of Martin and Katharina Luther. Here is what those who carefully observed their marriage would have learned.

Marriage Is Not a Matter of Compatibility but of Commitment

The truth is, Martin and Katharina barely knew each other

when they married. She had been living with a believing family in town and had been courted for nearly a year by a man who left town to marry someone else. This was followed by a brief courtship with a pastor she didn't like. In the meantime, Martin was living the life of a bachelor in the Black Cloister, immersed in his studies and writing.

He loved books and writing, and she loved farming and organizing and cleaning. One of the first things she did after their marriage was order two wagonloads of lime and whitewash the walls of the entire monastery. The monastery, or Black Cloister as it was called, was now empty of monks who had since left the Roman church. There were forty empty rooms, and the building was filthy.

In a typical marriage of Luther's day, the bride brought her bed into her new home, along with feather quilts and pillows and embroidered linens. But Katharina owned none of those things. Luther later revealed that their wedding night was spent on his bed, and he had not changed the rancid straw in it for over a year. He simply hadn't thought about it. He probably hadn't thought about a lot of things. As Luther wrote, "There is a lot to get used to in the first year of marriage."[196]

He noted years later, "Man has strange thoughts the first year of marriage. When sitting at table he thinks, 'Before I was alone; now there are two.' Or in bed, when he wakes up, he sees a pair of pigtails [on his pillow] which he hadn't seen there before."[197] Hello to married life. Everything about their lives had changed.

Luther observed, "Marriage does not always run smoothly ... one has to commit oneself to it."[198] Their marriage didn't work because they were compatible but because they were committed.

Marriage Is Not the Pursuit of Happiness but of Humility

Both Martin and Katharina were strong-willed, stubborn, opinionated, and extremely verbal. Luther admitted the revelation of his selfishness after marrying Katharina, writing, "Good Lord, what a lot of trouble there is in marriage. Adam has made a mess of our nature . . . marriage is [evidently] the school for character [development]."[199] That's true to this day. Marriage has the potential to reveal the worst about us and the best about us—sometimes in the same afternoon.

In Luther's day, the church taught that the monastery or nunnery was the training ground of virtue. Sequester a person away from everyone, and he or she will grow holy. Luther turned that entirely upside down, saying that marriage and family were the training grounds of virtue.[200] Marriage demands humility, change, and partnership.

Luther once wrote about fathers engaging in the help of raising children by physically entering into domestic chores that were typically reserved for the women. For instance, he wrote that men should not care if they are mocked for changing diapers or hanging them outdoors to dry after washing them. If the neighbors are amused, he said, "Let them laugh. God and the angels smile in heaven."[201] After all, this was, according to Luther, holy work.

Indeed, the Reformation made every vocation a sacred calling. Martin Luther viewed God as milking the cow through the milkmaid's hands. All work was a sacred calling. Katharina believed this as well and threw herself into serving her husband, family, and household. She arose so early in the morning to start work that Luther nicknamed her the Morning Star of Wittenberg.[202]

Life for Katharina and Martin never slowed down. On their wedding night a pastor seeking shelter banged on the door of the Black Cloister just after midnight. They welcomed him in as a guest. It was not long before all forty rooms once occupied by monks were occupied by out-of-town guests, students, professors, political and religious refugees, and nuns and monks who had escaped their religious orders.[203]

It took incredible humility to learn, not only to love and serve each other in the midst of all this, but also to serve so many people who invaded their lives uninvited. It must have been a special challenge for two people who, as a monk and a nun, had grown accustomed to lives of quiet solitude and privacy.

Soon they were raising six children, along with four nephews and nieces they adopted. This was in addition to running a forty-room hotel, a farm, a school, and a church. One author states that Katharina worked seventeen hours a day during the twenty-one years she was married to Martin Luther.[204] That's self-sacrificing humility on display.

The school of character was not found in the solitude of a monastery but in the busy chaos of marriage and family life.

Marriage Is Not an Antidote for Suffering but Opens a Door to Suffering

Katharina suffered incredibly painful attacks as a result of marrying Martin Luther. Everyone seemed to be against this marriage. From day one, the venom of the world was directed uniquely and particularly at Katharina. She was accused in pamphlets and letters that circulated throughout Germany of being a traitor to Christ for violating her vows as a nun. She was accused of being a "dancing girl" who had seduced a monk into marriage. The Catholic scholar Erasmus accused her of being with child when she married, having ensnared Martin by her seduction. Even though this was proven untrue, with the birth of their first child being a year after their marriage, the rumor never went away. In fact, there is an engraving made during their lifetime that depicts Martin and Katharina with their six children, but it also shows a seventh child lurking in the background.[205]

Just a year after their marriage, two church officials wrote letters telling Katharina to repent and return to the Mother Church or suffer the torments of hell. Luther could not resist responding, informing these officials that their letters had been used as toilet paper by the household servants.[206] That was classic Martin Luther.

Even King Henry VIII added his personal condemnation on their marriage, as if he were one to pass judgment on such matters! The king funded a play that mocked the marriage of a monk and a nun.[207]

Even as late as 1904, an 800-page biography of Martin Luther published by a Catholic historian portrayed Katharina as the reason Luther launched the Reformation. The author claimed Martin was simply trying to cover up what Katharina had made him do.[208]

It is difficult to imagine the impact this malicious slander had on this woman who merely wanted to serve her husband and, in so doing, to humbly and faithfully serve the Lord.

Marriage Is Not a Distraction from

Ministry but an Expansion of Ministry

Martin and Katharina's marriage became a partnership that, especially in their world, was incredibly unique and just as radical as the Reformation itself. For instance, Martin couldn't organize anything, a fact that evidenced itself in the home. In humility, he recognized this weakness and handed over all the finances, property, household purchases, and administration to Katharina. She proved to be a wonderful manager. He allowed her the freedom to purchase additional land and cattle, and she began to make money for their household needs. This was a revolutionary example to set!

Luther's well-known book, *Table Talk* wasn't actually written by him; rather, students and guests who gathered around his table in the evening collected his sayings and thoughts and published them. People in the sixteenth century ate two meals a day, the main dinner at midday and a simple meal at night. The word *supper* is derived from the tradition of serving soup, or "sops." It was over supper—or soup—that students asked questions and Luther responded. Debates would break out, and lively discussions would be held. It never would have happened had Katharina not prepared the soup for all these evening guests after taking care of all her many other household needs.

Katharina joined the conversation too. She did not leave after serving the meal. She stayed and also asked questions, entering into the debates with her own opinions. Students would marvel at this model of a husband and wife. Here was a husband and scholar who didn't confine his wife to the kitchen. She was a wife who engaged in the debates of the day.

Little known is that this gathering around the table at night was originally referred to by students as "Katy's table."[209] Without Katy, there never would have been *Table Talk*. Without Katy, there wouldn't have been any soup either. Katy's willingness to persevere in faith and commitment to Christ and to serve Martin allowed him to serve the world.

Katharina Luther is one of the unsung heroes of the Protestant Reformation. What a revolutionary model the home of Katharina and Martin Luther presented to those church leaders, students, and professors who passed through their doors. They saw a woman handling the finances and a man washing diapers, and they saw a husband and wife partnering in the gospel by using their home as a sanctuary and refuge.

Men and women left the Luther home profoundly impacted, and they took the Reformation of marriage, faith in action, partnership, love, loyalty, commitment, and humility around the world.

E. V. HILL AND S. M. LOCKRIDGE

When I was growing up, my father was a missionary to men and women in the military, so he frequently traveled to churches in the community that provided prayer and financial support to his ministry. He preached in all kinds of churches—Presbyterian, Methodist, Missionary Alliance, Baptist, and Brethren churches. In fact, every Sunday night, he would load our family into a bus full of sailors, and we would head to a church where he would preach.

One of the best memories I have from those days was a Sunday night when he preached in a church made up predominantly of African American believers. I had never seen a worship service quite like that before, and to this day it brings back fond memories. Nobody was sleeping in the pew! The service was riveting to me—from the opening announcement to the final benediction. It was, without a doubt, the most fun I'd ever had in church.

I was still taking piano lessons at that time, and I remember being blown away by the piano player. She was phenomenal. I vividly remember that upright piano. It was painted red, and I thought that was fitting, for as far as I could tell, it really was on fire. The music lifted you off your feet. It was wonderful.

To this day, I am particularly inspired and moved by the preaching of evangelical black pastors. I love bringing to my own congregation the preaching ministry of Richard Allen Farmer, Robert Smith, Charles Ware, and E. B. Charles.

Some of my favorite preachers today are African American pastors. Perhaps that is because I know they are standing on the shoulders of incredibly courageous fathers and grandfathers and great-grandfathers who remained faithful to Christ through much suffering.

I can't imagine how difficult it must have been for such men to pastor a church in America in 1860 or even 1960. So, when I hear or read their sermons about freedom in Christ and the faithfulness of God and the blessed hope of the Promised Land for God's people, there is something very rich and deep in their voices that I greatly admire.

Two of my favorite pastors from recent history—both of whom have been with the Lord now for nearly twenty years—are E. V. Hill and S. M. Lockridge.

Unfortunately, there are no biographies written on these men, but there is material available if you take the time to hunt for it. As I have read their sermons, listened to recordings of their preaching, and read whatever biographical information I could find, I have discovered that these two men lived with similar devotion and passion. Three traits they shared are worth remembering and imitating:

- What mattered to them was the gospel of Christ
- What motivated them was the approval of Christ
- What mesmerized them was the glory of Christ

E. V. Hill

E. V. Hill was born in 1933 in a log cabin in Texas. He was born into poverty and grew up in poverty. However, he would later say, "I really didn't know I was poor. [We] never equated materialism with poverty. Poverty was a matter of the spirit, and we were always rich in spirit."[210]

Through hard work and nothing short of the providence of

God, he graduated from high school and was given a scholarship to attend Prairie View Agricultural and Mechanical College for the Benefit of Colored Youth. How's that for the name of a college? The college had been chartered in the late 1800s to give the descendants of slaves the opportunity to attend college.

Hill's mother sacrificed greatly to purchase a bus ticket for him. When he arrived at the college, he had less than two dollars to his name. The college was not a theological or biblical training school, but it provided a valuable education to E. V. Hill.

At the age of twenty-one, Hill became pastor of a church in Texas. Seven years later, he moved to a church in Los Angeles. He served as a pastor for a total of forty-nine years. Though he lacked a formal theological education, Hill studied the Scriptures and preached them unapologetically with wisdom and power.

I recently listened to an audio recording of his sermon to several thousand pastors gathered in Moody Church in downtown Chicago. It is one of the best sermons I've ever heard on the power and glory of God.

Reading about E. V. Hill's life took me back to Luke's words in Acts 4:13 in reference to Peter and John. I believe this verse also gives in one sentence an accurate description of E. V. Hill and his ministry.

Acts 4:13 says: "Now as they [the Sanhedrin] observed the confidence of Peter and John and understood that they were uneducated and untrained men, they were amazed, and began to recognize them as having been with Jesus."

"Confidence" translates a word that "carries the idea of expressing oneself without holding anything back."[211] The Sanhedrin is trying to shut them down, but the apostles won't quit.

Here Peter and John are speaking with confidence to Israel's Supreme Court (the Sanhedrin), delivering the truth about Jesus Christ. And they aren't holding anything back.

The Sanhedrin—no doubt some of the most biblically educated men in Israel—are stunned. The word for "uneducated" literally means unlettered. The word for "untrained" means unschooled.[212]

Notice again what Luke writes next: "They were amazed, and began to recognize them as having been with Jesus." The only conclusion the Sanhedrin can draw is that the powerful ministry of these men had nothing to do with education but, rather, association. They had been with Jesus!

Maybe the reason we aren't having the spiritual fruit we would like to have, despite being more educated than ever, is because the world isn't recognizing us as having been with Jesus.

What is clear from E. V. Hill's ministry is that he cared more about his association with Jesus than anything else. He would be disliked by people from the white community, the black community, and every other community simply because when he spoke the truth, he did not hold anything back.

I found it interesting that E. V. Hill is not listed as one of the notable alumni of *Prairie View* on its Wikipedia page. On that list of notable alumni are the names of corporate CEOs, university presidents, professional athletes, and elected officials, along with the names of recording artists and concert musicians and civil rights leaders. But the most famous pastor to have graduated from that school is not listed. If you study his life and listen to his preaching, however, you can understand why.

- He placed the gospel above racial issues.
- He was more interested in building the church than a political party.
- He had close friendships with people like Martin Luther King Jr. (to whom he was a confidant) and Jerry Falwell.
- He preached a pro-life, six-day-creation message.
- He left the Democratic Party and began identifying with conservative political leaders.
- He prayed at the inauguration of one Republican president and become a key mentor to another conservative president.
- He once called the American Civil Liberties Union "satanic."

One thing was clear: Edward Victor Hill delivered the gospel of right and wrong and heaven and hell, and he didn't hold anything back. What mattered to him was the gospel of Christ, and what motivated him was the approval of Christ.

In his book on Christians and politics, James Montgomery Boice commends the gospel centrality of E. V. Hill's mission, illustrating how his church, Mount Zion Missionary Baptist Church, impacted the Los Angeles area for Christ.

At one time early in his ministry, E. V. had served as a ward leader for the Democratic Party before switching allegiances to support conservative Republican politicians. As a ward leader, his assignment was to raise votes for the Democratic candidates, and his chief strategy for doing this was to enroll a block captain for each block of his ward. On election day, he told these captains to encourage every resident on their block to get out and vote.

When E. V. Hill came to Los Angeles, he was convicted by the thought that if he had been such a good missionary for the Democrats, why shouldn't he be one for the Lord? Why not have a Christian block captain for every block of Los Angeles? There were 3,100 blocks in that area at that time, but Hill was up to the task and that became his church's mission.

Boice wrote that when He first heard E. V. talk about this goal, the church had already elected captains in 1,900 blocks. Church members were strategically moving from their homes, stationing themselves as block missionaries. They had adopted Hill's conviction that they existed for the sake of proclaiming and spreading the gospel.

E. V. Hill tells of a funny thing that happened on one occasion. One man became annoyed by the block captain where he lived. Day after day, she invited him to church and talked to him about the Lord. She was friendly but persistent. So, he decided to move to the other side of Los Angeles.

The moving truck came. He loaded up his possessions. His block captain came out to say good-bye to him. He didn't say all that much in return; he was probably thinking, *I'm glad to finally get away from you people!*

As soon as the moving truck was out of sight, the block captain ran into the house, got out the directory of the Mount Zion block captains, and dialed the person in charge of the block to which her neighbor was moving. As soon as he pulled up to his new residence, his new block captain was there to welcome him and invite him to church! His response was classic: "You people are everywhere!"[213]

Upon reading that story, I was deeply convicted. What could we do if we truly believed that we were called to *this* city, at *this* time, in *this* generation, to deliver to every person the gospel of Jesus Christ? E. V. Hill gives us a picture of what that would look like, and it is worth imitating.

S. M. Lockridge

A colleague of E. V. Hill who grew up equally passionate about the gospel was Shadrach Meshach Lockridge. He was born in 1913 and lived to the end of that century. Again, there is no biography on his life and much less information is available on him than on E. V. Hill. The facts we do know, however, are intriguing.

S. M. Lockridge grew up in the depression days of the Midwest. Like E. V. Hill, his first church was in Texas. Eventually, he moved to California in 1952, where he was called to be the pastor of Calvary Baptist Church in San Diego. He would serve in that church for some forty years. He died in 2000 at the age of eighty-seven.

While pastoring in California, he became a powerful religious and social voice, especially in San Diego. He also became the president of the California Missionary Baptist State Convention and was known for his courageous and powerful preaching. Like E. V. Hill, S. M. Lockridge developed a reputation for declaring what he believed and holding nothing back.

Later in his ministry, he served on the faculty of the Billy Graham School of Evangelism and the Greater Los Angeles Sunday School Convention. He published, *Rekindling the Holy Fires* and *The Lordship of Christ*. He also preached at crusades, evangelistic rallies, and conferences all around the world.

Colleagues called him a giant among preachers, and if you've ever heard him preach, you would agree. His best-known message is a sermon entitled "That's my King!" His unforgettable descriptions serve as a moving exaltation of the glory of Christ.

To date, this sermon has been downloaded millions of

times from the internet and has become one of the most listened-to sermons in the modern church age. Here are some excerpts from that sermon:

The Bible says...

My King is the King of the Jews....
He's the King of Israel....
He's the King of Righteousness.
He's the King of the Ages.
He's the King of Heaven.
He's the King of Glory.
He's the King of Kings, and He's the Lord of Lords.
Now, that's my King. Well, I wonder, if you know Him?...

He's the greatest phenomenon
That ever crossed the horizon of this world.
He's God's Son.
He's the sinner's Savior.
He's the centerpiece of civilization....
He's unparalleled.
He's unprecedented....
He sympathizes and He saves.
He strengthens and sustains.
He guards and He guides....
He forgives sinners.
He discharges debtors....
He serves the unfortunate.
He regards the aged.
And He rewards the diligent....
Do you know Him?...

His light is matchless.
His goodness is limitless.
His mercy is everlasting.

His love never changes.
His Word is enough.
His grace is sufficient.
His reign is righteous.
And His yoke is easy,
And his burden is light.

I wish I could describe Him to you, but
He's indescribable.
He's incomprehensible....
You can't get Him out of your mind.
You can't get Him off of your hands.
You can't out live Him,
and you can't live without Him.

The Pharisees couldn't stand Him,
but they found out they couldn't stop Him.
Pilate couldn't find any fault in Him....
And Herod couldn't kill Him.
Death couldn't handle Him,
and the grave couldn't hold Him.
That's my King![214]

❖ ❖ ❖

E. V. Hill and S. M. Lockridge are worthy of imitation, not because of their oratory or politics or the size of their congregations. They are worthy because what mattered to them was the gospel of Christ, what motivated them was the approval of Christ, and what mesmerized them was the glory of Christ.

DR. VIGGO OLSEN

The *New York Times* called Viggo Olsen another David Livingstone, for like Livingstone, Olsen served as a medical missionary in uncharted territory. Dr. Olsen also served as a diplomatic leader, statesman, pioneering church planter, and Bible translator while serving in Bangladesh, a predominantly Muslim country recently formed on the eastern border of India.

I have long been interested in Viggo Olsen's life and ministry, and not just because of his fascinating autobiography entitled *Daktar*, which is Bengali for *doctor*.[215] I have had a personal interest in this servant of the Lord because a member of my own extended family, a third cousin, Becky Davey, served as a missionary nurse alongside Dr. Olsen for decades. I can still remember Becky visiting our home when I was a young boy. She wore a colorful Sari and a winsome smile as she shared stories about the hospital and the ministry among the teeming masses of people in Bangladesh.

Spiritual Journey

As a young medical student, Viggo Olsen, known as Vic by his friends, was a brilliant agnostic who was convinced that his evolutionary worldview answered the fundamental questions of origins. He considered Christianity just one among many religions and the Christian worldview somewhat backward and unintelligent.

But then something happened. It dramatically changed his life, to the point that he eventually refused an invitation to join the medical team at the Mayo Clinic and turned down other prestigious opportunities in the medical field, including the offer to become the chief surgeon at one of America's largest hospitals.

That influential event occurred early in his marriage to his wife Joan. Though Viggo and Joan were both agnostic, her parents had become committed followers of Christ. One night, even though a friendly debate left Viggo boiling with anger inside, he and Joan accepted her parents' challenge to personally investigate the claims of Jesus Christ. Olsen was convinced it would not take much time to debunk what he called "an unscientific religion" and prove Christianity false. Besides, he had already been fully immersed in evolution and the belief that

God was essentially the creation of people's imaginations because they feared death and the unknown.

To Olsen, the idea that God created the universe and designed the human body, the animal kingdom, and everything else on the planet was utter foolishness. It was insulting to any thoughtful person, and especially to a brilliant medical student.

He had been raised during the heady days of scientific advancement. When he was in elementary school, in the 1930s, the respected minds of the scientific world were becoming bolder in their denunciations of the Genesis account of creation. One famous British astronomer declared that "the notion of a beginning was repugnant." The scientific community applauded his bravado. And by far the most famous mind at the time when Olsen was entering high school was the brilliant Albert Einstein, who said in an interview, "The circumstance of an initial moment of creation irritates me."[216]

The apostle Paul said it *would* be irritating. In fact, the Bible informs us that the knowledge of divine creation is so troubling to the God-denying world that they actively seek to banish this truth from their thoughts. Romans 1:18-20 tells us that while the power and nature of God is clearly revealed by what He has created, unbelieving humanity suppresses this truth, which is evident in them and to them.

When Paul said they "suppress the truth," he used a verb that means to hold down or stifle. Unbelievers do not want the truth about God known—to themselves or others. In nautical contexts, this same word has the meaning of "to steer towards."[217] And so it is that no matter what they see or what they observe or what they discover, the world is going to interpret it in a way that keeps steering people away from the idea that God had something to do with it and instead steer them toward the idea that God is absent and unneeded.

That is where Viggo Olsen and his young wife were and where they were determined to stand. Nonetheless, they politely agreed to study the claims of Christ and the Bible, assuming it wouldn't take much to defend evolution and prove that Christ was only a good man and Christianity just another man-made religion.

They began their investigation by attempting to disprove the concept of creation. Olsen wrote,

> *Scientifically we knew that the planet earth and its universe had not always existed. . . . which meant they must have been created by some mighty force or power.*

> *"But what proof is there that a power brought it into being?" Joan asked.*

> "Because," I answered, "our earth and universe are packed with power—fire power, water power, atomic energy, etc. Only a power or energy can bring into being a power-packed system."
>
> "But was this an intelligent power or was it some undirected, cosmic explosion?" we asked ourselves.[218]

As a medical student, Olsen was exposed to the patterns of cells. He could study tissue under the microscope and determine whether it was lung tissue or brain tissue or heart tissue simply because of the patterns. He wrote:

> We could not find a design without a designer or a pattern without a pattern-maker. And there was unquestionable evidence of pattern and design in our universe and on our planet. The millions of stars and planets track their orbits precisely ... Without fail, the earth and sun maintain their correct relationship so that we live out our lives without being burned to a crisp or frozen into a cosmic ice cube.[219]

He began to see that everywhere there is proof of an intelligent power that brought everything into being.

No doubt it was the work of the Spirit of God, who was in the process of opening his eyes to the truth of God's Word, that led Viggo and Joan to an analogy that gave them "valuable perspective." They considered what would happen if they placed the wooden blocks from one hundred Scrabble games into a covered plastic tub, shook the letters, and then threw the thousands of pieces out onto the floor. Would they fall so that the letters formed a story or a poem? No. Some would lie on top of others, and many would rest face down, upside down, or sideways, but they would not form even a single paragraph.

But suppose someone with fingers connected to an intelligent mind picked up the scattered pieces and formed them into words and sentences so that a story emerged from the heaps of wooden blocks. Viggo wrote:

> *Power shook the tub and threw the pieces upon the floor. Another power carefully picked up the pieces and with them told the story. Then why the difference in the two results? We saw immediately that the difference lies in the types of power involved. The first power, undirected, failed to produce a pattern from the blocks; the second power, intelligent power, produced the pattern we can read as a story.*[220]

Viggo Olsen and his wife came to believe the truth of David's great declaration in Psalm 19:1: "The heavens are telling of the glory of God; and their expanse [i.e., the sky and the planets and stars and galaxies around us] is declaring the work of His hands." The Hebrew verbs for "telling" and "declaring" in this verse are correctly understood as continuous. In other words, the message of the heavens never turns off. Psalm 19:1 could be translated, "The heavens keep on telling us about the glory of God, and the sky keeps on describing for us His handiwork."[221]

Creation is the handiwork of God—that is, His hand-work. Like a sculptor or an artist, God has crafted and then signed creation with His signature.

Pablo Picasso, the famed modern artist, reportedly rolled

his thumb in the paint and then rolled it on the canvas as his signature on a number of paintings. In Psalm 19, David essentially says that if you take the time to look, God's fingerprints are everywhere! His artistry is on continuous display all around the planet.

Eugene Petersen, in *The Message*, paraphrases this opening line wonderfully: "God's glory is on tour in the skies."

Psalm 19 continues, "Day to day pours forth speech, and night to night reveals knowledge" (Psalm 19:2). "Pours forth speech" translates a Hebrew word meaning to gush forth, as from a bubbling spring of water; it just keeps bubbling up more information about the creative power of God.

Notice that this is taking place "day to day," or literally day after day after day after day. The brilliant wisdom of God just keeps bubbling up out of His creation. And it isn't just day after day. David adds, it is also "night to night." Turn the lights out, and an entirely new photo album of knowledge about the creative genius and glory of God appears in the sky above.

The word David used at the end of verse 2 for "knowledge" can be understood to mean "observable data."[222] Day after day and night after night, the observable data of creation is constantly bubbling up knowledge about our God and His creation.

So where would you like to look? Study the petals of a flower. Study the animals around you. Study the human body.

It is all amazing. As Viggo Olsen began to look around and connect the dots, whether it was the patterns of cellular structure, the laws of nature, the beauty and hospitality of planet earth providing drinkable water, the precision of gravity, or the nature of light, all the data that kept bubbling up gave more and more reasons to acknowledge and praise the Creator God.[223]

Olsen was given a book written by a collection of evangelical scientists concerning truths that had been suppressed but were now exposed to the light of day. He wrote that his polite interest grew into a passionate fascination. It wasn't long before Olsen and his wife settled in their minds the reality of a Creator God.

Upon being convinced of a Creator, however, the Olsens next attempted to disprove the consistency and reliability of Scripture. But Viggo Olsen wrote:

> *Despite its sixty-six books, written over sixteen hundred years by over forty authors (some of them peasants and fisherman; others, kings, physicians, and poets), the Bible books harmonized as though one person had written them all.[224]*

In college he had been taught that writing was unknown in Moses' time and that the Hittites and Edomites mentioned in the Bible were legends. Yet he learned that modern archeological research had upended every one of those theories. Writing was discovered to be an art during the days of Moses, as well as in days of his forefather Abraham, and even hundreds of years earlier. The Hittite civilization was discovered and excavated. And the ancient Edomite culture, once denied as a biblical myth, had captivated the imagination of the world as tourists could now visit its magnificent city of Petra with its beautiful buildings, theaters, and homes carved into the limestone cliffs.[225]

In the process of their investigation, Olsen and his wife also turned to the prophecies of Scripture and learned that more than thirty prophetic utterances were fulfilled on the day of Christ's crucifixion. They originally viewed Jesus as simply a remarkable man, a martyr for His cause, but the evidence of fulfilled prophecies stirred Olsen to wonder aloud to his wife whether Jesus was God's means of communicating with mankind. He had already studied Plato, who claimed that philosophy could in no way deny the possibility of divine revelation.[226]

So, did God reveal Himself to us? As they studied the Gospel accounts, Olsen admitted that God was clearly communicating with mankind. In fact, he told his wife on one occasion, that to communicate successfully with an ant, he would have to become an ant; so the argument followed perfectly that for God to communicate effectively with us, He would have to join the human race.[227] And with that, the words of John struck a deep chord in them: "In the beginning was the Word, and the Word was with God, and the Word was God. . . . And the Word became flesh, and dwelt among us, and we saw His glory" (John 1:1, 14).

God sent His *logos*, His "Word" or explanation, and His explanation came through His Son, Jesus Christ. And yet the "Word" is also God.

Dr. Olsen and his wife were edging closer to the conclusion that Jesus Christ is God in human form. They began to study His stupendous claims that He was "the resurrection and the life" (John 11:25) and that He alone could lead us from life, through death, into eternal life—that He was "the way, and the truth, and the life," the entry point into heaven itself (John 14:1-6).

Olsen wrote, "The resurrection of Christ was to us the hinge or crux of the whole question of the deity of Christ. If He *did* rise from the dead, we would have to grant that Jesus is the Son of God . . . [and] that all Jesus ever said is true and binding."[228]

The Olsens studied the eyewitness accounts of the resurrection of Jesus, noting that all of them were consistent in their reporting. The change in His disciples was radical. When

Jesus was in the tomb, the disciples had hidden away, huddled together in a room, terrified to do anything or say anything. But after they claimed to have seen and talked with their resurrected Lord, every one of them suddenly became bold and courageous. Even though it meant that most of them would face horrible executions in the years ahead, the disciples never backed away from their testimony.

Dr. Olsen wrote that his "invincible" agnostic arguments were crumbling, yet he didn't know how to relate to God. He had assumed Christianity, like other religions, taught that if a person lived a decent life and avoided hurting others, the good deeds would cancel out the bad and put one on good terms with God in the end.[229]

Viggo and Joan kept studying the Scriptures. As they did, they encountered verse after verse that showed Christianity to be distinct from every other religion. They discovered it was not a religion of good works and self-help but a relationship entered into by repentance and faith in the Lord Jesus Christ.

Verses like these arrested their attention:

- "He saved us, not on the basis of deeds which we have done in righteousness, but according to His mercy." (Titus 3:5)
- "God . . . has saved us and called us with a holy calling, not according to our works, but according to His own purpose and grace." (2 Timothy 1:8-9)
- "'Believe in the Lord Jesus, and you will be

saved.'" (Acts 16:31)
- "But as many as have received Him [Christ], to them He gave the right to become children of God." (John 1:12)
- "'Whoever will call on the name of the Lord will be saved.'" (Romans 10:13)

Viggo and Joan Olsen called upon the name of the Lord—and their lives would never be the same.

Ministry and Advice

The Olsens went on to serve in Bangladesh, making disciples, planting churches, and building a hospital. They served royal families, as well as poor beggars, providing medical and spiritual help and giving people answers to the questions they themselves once asked, questions human hearts and minds everywhere in the world still ask:

- Where did the earth and universe come from?
- Did God communicate with mankind?
- Is the Bible reliable?
- Where can a person find forgiveness from sin?
- How can a person have eternal life?

With a long and spiritually prosperous ministry in Bangladesh, Viggo Olsen has left us a lasting example of faithfulness to God. He has also left us some valuable advice. Viggo's brilliant clinical mind and his own experience helped him develop a very profound, yet simple four-step procedure for making decisions as one seeks to obey God and follow Him.

Erase and Pray

The first step in Olsen's decision-making process is *erase and pray*. In other words, make a conscious mental effort to erase your own desires, as though you were erasing a blackboard clean, so that God can imprint upon your mental chalkboard His will for you. Then pray, asking God to finish the erasing process and give you wisdom.

Read and Remember

Second, read Scripture because there God has not only revealed Himself but also revealed His will about numerous matters. Purchase a concordance to look up Scripture by topic or key word. Saturate your mind with the truth of God's Word as you erase, pray, read, and remember what God has already revealed.

Consider and Think

Next, write down available options regarding the decision you need to make. Consider them carefully. Draw a line down a piece of paper, and list all the pros and cons. Gather the advice and counsel of mature Christians. Think through the various aspects of your decision, and consider the circumstances and the consequences of each choice.

Decide and Check

Finally, check your heart and mind for a sense of God's pleasure and peace as you move forward. Then make a decision and act in faith, trusting that God would have led you differently if it were His will.

If you are still undecided, go back and start again with the first step: erase and pray.[230]

Viggo Olsen used to teach the Bengali believers as he discipled them that God's plan for their lives was not like a blueprint laid out on a drawing board with every detail visible at one glance. It was more like a scroll, unrolled bit by bit to reveal His plan for their lives. He told them, "Unrolling your scroll completely will take a lifetime."[231]

That's great advice. Maybe for you today it is time to seriously consider the claims of Jesus Christ and His gospel. Perhaps it is time to ask God to open your eyes to creation and to search the Bible for answers.

If you are a believer, perhaps Viggo Olsen's perspective and advice are worth imitating. You may want God to send you a blueprint of your life, but He wants to unroll the scroll of your life just one inch at a time, as you make thoughtful, godly decisions each step of the way.

If God is capable enough and wise enough to design a universe to work according to His purpose, He's capable and wise enough to direct your steps—and, eventually, lead you all the way home.

ENDNOTES

[1] John Philips, Exploring Psalms: Volume Two (Loizeaux Brothers, 1988), 478.

[2] Aggie Hurst, Aggie: The Inspiring Story of a Girl Without a Country (Access Publishing, 1986). This book is the primary source for the story recounted here.

[3] Ibid., 97.

[4] Ibid., 114.

[5] Ibid., 120-25.

[6] Dan Graves, "Amy Carmichael, Kindly Kidnapper," christianity.com.

[7] "Amy Carmichael," womenofchristianity.com.

[8] Frank L. Houghton, Amy Carmichael of Dohnavur (CLC, 1953), 138.

[9] See Warren W. Wiersbe, 50 People Every Christian Should Know (Baker Books, 2009), 299.

[10] Houghton, 324.

[11] Amy Carmichael, "Make Me Thy Fuel, Flame of God."

[12] A. W. Tozer, The Root of the Righteous (Moody Press, 2015), 189.

[13] James L. Snyder, The Life of A. W. Tozer (Regal, 2009), 109.

[14] Warren W. Wiersbe, 50 People Every Christian Should Know (Baker Books, 2009), 352.

[15] "A. W. Tozer," The Alliance. cmalliance.org.

[16] A. W. Tozer, Reclaiming Christianity: A Call to Authentic Faith, compiled and edited by James L. Snyder (Regal, 2009), 10.

[17] A. W. Tozer, The Knowledge of the Holy (Harper/San Francisco, 1961), 6.

[18] This story is recounted by James L. Snyder in his introduction to Reclaiming Christianity, 8.

[19] Tozer, Reclaiming Christianity, 10.

[20] The original source for this quote could not be located.

[21] Steven Lawson, Heaven Help Us! (Navpress, 1995), 22.

[22] A. W. Tozer, Of God and Men (Christian Publications, 1960), 34.

[23] Ibid., 32.

[24] A. W. Tozer, The Dangers of a Shallow Faith, compiled and edited by James L. Snyder (Bethany House, 2012), 23.

[25] These words are commonly and widely attributed to Tozer. The original source could not be located.

[26] James L. Snyder, "A Profile in Devotion," awtozerclassics.com

[27] Ibid.

[28] Ibid.

[29] Robert J. Morgan, Nelson's Complete Book of Stories, Illustrations and Quotes (Thomas Nelson, 2000), 465.

[30] A. W. Tozer, The Knowledge of the Holy (HarperCollins, 1961), 1.

[31] Ibid., 56.

[32] James Boice, Psalms: An Expositional Commentary, Volume 3 (Baker Books, 1998), 1202.

[33] Dan Edelen, "Review—A Passion for God: The Spiritual Journey of A. W. Tozer," ceruleansanctum.com

[34] Tim Challies, "A. W. Tozer: A Passion for God," challis.com, February 17, 2011.

[35] Warren W. Wiersbe, A Treasury of Tozer (Baker Book House, 1980), 7.

[36] A. W. Tozer, The Pursuit of God (Christian Publications, 1993), 19-20.

[37] Diana Lynn Severance, Feminine Threads: Women in the Tapestry of Christian History (Christian Focus Publications, 2011), 212.

[38] Anne Adams, "Susanna Wesley: Mother of Methodism," History's Women, historyswomen.com/womenoffaith/SusannahWesley.html

[39] Ingvar Haddal, John Wesley (Abingdon Press, 1961), 15.

[40] Diane Hopkins, "Oh Susanna!" Love to Learn, lovetolearn.net

[41] Ibid.

[42] Ibid.

[43] Adams.

[44] Haddal, 20.

[45] Hopkins.

[46] The summary of the Wesleys' marriage and family life in this section is taken primarily from Beverly Whitaker, "Susanna Wesley," freepages.rootsweb.com/~gentutor/genealogy/susanna.html

[47] Severance, 214.

[48] Adams.

[49] Ibid.

[50] "Oswald Chambers Biography," Oswald Chambers Publication Association, oswaldchambers.co.uk.

[51] Warren W. Wiersbe, 50 People Every Christian Should Know (Baker Books, 2009), 321.

[52] David McCasland, Oswald Chambers: Abandoned to God (Discovery House, 1993), 214.

[53] See Wiersbe, 321.

[54] "Oswald Chambers Biography."

[55] McCasland, 214.

[56] John MacArthur, The MacArthur New Testament Commentary: Luke 11-17 (Moody Publishers, 2013), 54.

[57] William Barclay, The Gospel of Luke (Westminster Press, 1975), 146.

[58] See MacArthur, 57.

[59] The Quotable Oswald Chambers, compiled and edited by David McCasland (Discovery House, 2008), 93, 94.

[60] Wiersbe, 320.

[61] McCasland, Oswald Chambers, 159.

[62] Quoted at Christian Classics Ethereal Library, "Oswald Chambers," ccel.org/ccel/chambers.html.

[63] McCasland, Oswald Chambers, 247.

[64] Wiersbe, 323.

[65] Ibid.

[66] Ibid.

[67] The Quotable Oswald Chambers, 10.

[68] Wiersbe, 326.

[69] The Quotable Oswald Chambers, 97.

[70] Adoniram Judson, "Advice to Missionary Candidates," wholesomewords.org.

[71] "Adoniram Judson," Gfamissions.org.

[72] John Piper, Adoniram Judson: How Few There Are Who Die So Hard, ebook (Desiring God Foundation, 2012), 11.

[73] Ibid.

[74] Ibid., 12.

[75] Ibid., quoting Courtney Anderson, To the Golden Shore: The Life of Adoniram Judson (Zondervan, 1956).

[76] Jesse Clement, Memoir of Adoniram Judson: Being a Sketch of His Life and Missionary Labors (Derby and Miller, 1853), 25.

[77] Piper, 13.

[78] Clement, 170.

[79] Piper, 18, quoting Anderson.

[80] "Adoniram Judson," gfamissions.org.

[81] Harry Ignatius Marshall, The Karen People of Burma: A Study in Anthropology and Ethnology, ebook (Reprint; Project Gutenberg Australia, 2009), Gutenberg.net.au. See also "Adoniram Judson," wikipedia.org.

[82] "Adoniram Judson: Missionary," wholesomewords.org.

[83] Ibid.

[84] Fred Barlow, "Adoniram Judson: Father of Baptist Missionaries," wholesomewords.org.

[85] Ibid.

[86] Piper, 7-8.

[87] Galen B. Royer, "Adoniram Judson: Burma's First Missionary," wholesomewords.org.

[88] Kenneth O. Gangel, Holman New Testament Commentary: John (Holman, 2000), 189.

[89] Ibid.

[90] James Montgomery Boice, The Gospel of John (Zondervan, 1985), 604.

[91] Ibid.

[92] "Frances Jane Crosby," earnestlycontending.com

[93] Warren W. Wiersbe, 50 People Every Christian Should Know (Baker Books, 2009), 102.

[94] See Wiersbe, 101.

[95] Ibid., 103.

[96] Darlene Neptune, Fanny Crosby Still Lives (Pelican, 2001), 67.

[97] J. M. K., "Safe in the Arms of Jesus," wholesomewords.org.

[98] Ibid.

[99] William Barclay, Letters to the Corinthians (Westminster, 1975), 210.

[100] Ibid.

[101] New Tribes Mission is today known as Ethnos 360.

[102] Auca was the name they were known by among outsiders. They are more properly known as Waodani, or Waorani.

[103] This is not a precise quote. The words are taken from Elisabeth Elliot's radio program and are recorded here from memory.

[104] Steve Saint, End of the Spear (Tyndale, 2005), 34-35.

[105] Ibid., 58.

[106] Elisabeth Elliot, Suffering Is Never for Nothing (B&H Publishing, 2019), Electronic edition.

[107] "Elisabeth Elliot & Rachel Saint," thetravelingteam.org.

[108] Steve Saint, "Did They Have to Die?" Christianity Today, September 16, 1996.

[109] Dr. and Mrs. Howard Taylor, Hudson Taylor in Early Years: The Growth of a Soul (OMF International, 1996), 67

[110] Ibid., 136-37.

[111] Ibid., 134.

[112] Ibid.

[113] Ibid., 135.

[114] Ibid.

[115] Dr. and Mrs. Howard Taylor, J. Hudson Taylor: God's Man in China (Moody Press, 1965), 99.

[116] Alexander Strauch, Leading with Love (Lewis and Roth, 2006), 61.

[117] Dr. and Mrs. Howard Taylor, Hudson Taylor and the China Inland Mission: The Growth of a Work of God (Morgan and Scott, 1918), 31.

[118] Ibid., 318.

[119] J. Oswald Sanders, Spiritual Leadership: Principles of Excellence for Every Believer (Moody, 2007), 136.

[120] Taylor, Hudson Taylor and the China Inland Mission: The Growth of a Work of God, 276.

[121] Ibid., 226-27.

[122] Ibid., 230.

[123] R. Kent Hughes, 1001 Great Stories and Quotes (Tyndale House, 1998), 213.

[124] Ibid., 493.

[125] John Dunn, A Biography of John Newton (New Creation Teaching Ministry), 1.

[126] E. J. A., Bright Examples: Short Sketches of Christian Life (Dublin Tract Repository, n.d.), 12.

[127] Dunn, 8.

[128] Dunn, 9.

[129] John Piper, The Roots of Endurance (Crossway, 2002), 47.

[130] Ibid., 48

[131] An untitled hymn from Newton and William Cowper's Olney Hymns; quoted in Bright Examples, 24.

[132] Dunn, 16.

[133] Ibid., 29.

[134] Ibid., 17.

[135] Ibid., 20.

[136] Ibid., 29.

[137] Ibid.

[138] Bright Examples, 49.

[139] John Pollock, Amazing Grace: John Newton's Story (Harper & Row, 1981), 182.

[140] Bright Examples, 50.

[141] Vance Christie, Timeless Stories: God's Incredible Work in the Lives of Inspiring Christians

(Christian Focus, 2012), 12.

[142] "Charles H. Spurgeon," Short Biography, A Baptist Page Portrait, wholesomewords.com.

[143] Harry C. Howard, "A Root Out of Dry Ground," wholesomewords.com.

[144] F. W. Boreham, "C. H. Spurgeon's Text," wholesomewords.com.

[145] C. H. Spurgeon, Autobiography: Volume 1 (Banner of Truth Trust reprint, 2006), 180.

[146] R. Kent Hughes, The Sermon on the Mount (Crossway Books, 2001), 26.

[147] Spurgeon, Autobiography, Volume 1, 145.

[148] Bob L. Ross, A Pictorial Biography of C. H. Spurgeon (Pilgrim Publications, 1974), 66.

[149] Richard Ellsworth Day, The Shadow of the Broad Brim (Judson Press, 1934), 110.

[150] Spurgeon, Autobiography, Volume 1, 289.

[151] Ibid., 3.

[152] Quoted in John Piper, A Camaraderie of Confidence (Crossway, 2016), 42.

[153] Quoted in ibid., 43.

[154] C. H. Spurgeon, Autobiography: Volume 2 (Banner of Truth Trust reprint, 2006), 162.

[155] C. H. Spurgeon, Lectures to My Students (Hendrickson Publishers, 2010), 34-35.

[156] W. Y. Fullerton, Charles Spurgeon: A Biography (CreateSpace, 2014), 151.

[157] Charles Spurgeon, The Suffering of Man and the Sovereignty of God (Fox River Press, 2001), 18.

[158] Quoted in John Piper, Charles Spurgeon: Preaching Through Adversity (Desiring God, 2015), 18.

[159] R. Kent Hughes, Romans (Crossway Books, 1991), 263.

[160] Charles H. Spurgeon, Morning and Evening (Hendrickson Publishers, 1991), 534.

[161] Timothy George, "Big Picture Faith," Christianity Today, September 23, 2000.

[162] New Webster's Dictionary and Thesaurus (Lexicon Publications, 1995), 1003.

[163] J. Gilchrist Lawson, "George Müller," wholesomewords.com

[164] Ibid.

[165] John Piper, "George Mueller's Strategy for Showing God," desiringgod.org, February 3, 2004.

[166] Arthur T. Pierson, George Müller of Bristol: His Life of Prayer and Faith (Kregel, 1999), 274.

[167] Quoted in Piper.

[168] Ibid.

[169] Roger Steer, George Müller: Delighted in God (Harold Shaw Publishers, 1981), 161.

[170] Quoted in Piper.

[171] Pierson, 274.

[172] Wayne Grudem, Systematic Theology (Zondervan, 1994), 1252.

[173] John Piper, The Hidden Smile of God (Crossway Books, 2001), 85.

[174] Ibid, 86.

[175] T. S. Grimshawe, ed., William Cowper: His Life, Letters, and Poems (Crosby, Nichols, Lee and Company, 1860), 476.

[176] Piper, 89.

[177] Marion Harland, William Cowper (G. P. Putnam's Sons, 1899), 53.

[178] "God Moves in a Mysterious Way." In the original Olney Hymns, it is titled "Light Shining out of Darkness."

[179] Harland, 90.

[180] Harland, 90; George Melvyn Ella, William Cowper: Poet of Paradise (Evangelical Press, 1993), 186.

[181] Harland, 90.

[182] Robert Southey, ed., The Works of William Cowper (Baldwin and Craddock, 1836), 226.

[183] Warren W. Wiersbe, Victorious Christians You Should Know (Baker Book House, 1984), 95.

[184] Michelle DeRusha, Katharina and Martin Luther: The Radical Marriage of a Runaway Nun and a Renegade Monk (Baker Books, 2017), 47.

[185] Ibid., 51.

[186] Ibid., 54.

[187] Ibid., 80.

[188] Quoted in R. C. Sproul, Faith Alone (Baker Books), 56.

[189] DeRusha, 91.

[190] Ibid., 94.

[191] Quoted in Sproul, 56.

[192] DeRusha, 134.

[193] Wiersbe, 96.

[194] DeRusha, 150.

[195] Wiersbe, 97.

[196] Quoted in Wiersbe, 98.

[197] Eric Metaxas, Martin Luther (Viking, 2017), 352.

[198] Quoted in DeRusha, 273.

[199] Quoted in Wiersbe, 99.

[200] Roland H. Bainton, Here I Stand (Abington Press, 1978), 307.

[201] Quoted in Bainton, 308.

[202] DeRusha, 178

[203] Ibid.

[204] Ibid., 190.

[205] Ibid., 169.

[206] Ibid., 173.

[207] Ruth A. Tucker, Katie Luther: First Lady of the Reformation (Zondervan, 2017), 78.

[208] Ibid., 167.

[209] DeRusha, 201.

[210] Larry B. Stammer, "E.V. Hill, 69; Longtime L.A. Pastor Was National Civil Rights, Religious Leader," Los Angeles Times, February 26, 2003, latimes.com.

[211] Everett F. Harrison, Acts: The Expanding Church (Moody Press, 1975), 84.

[212] R. Kent Hughes, Acts: The Church Afire (Crossway Books, 1996), 64.

[213] James Montgomery Boice, Two Cities, Two Loves (InterVarsity Press, 1996), 168.

[214] S. M. Lockridge, "That's My King," youtube.com; "That's My King! Do You Know Him?" shadowmountain.org.

[215] Viggo Olsen, Daktar: Diplomat in Bangladesh (Moody Press, 1973).

[216] John MacArthur, The Battle for the Beginning (W Publishing, 2001), 164.

[217] Gerhard Kittle, ed., Theological Dictionary of the New Testament, trans. Geoffrey W. Bromiley (Eerdmans, 1964), 2:829.

[218] Olsen, 40.

[219] Ibid.

[220] Ibid., 41.

[221] William VanGemeren, "Psalms," in The Expositor's Bible Commentary, ed. Frank E. Gaebelein (Zondervan, 1991), 5:179.

[222] G. A. F. Knight, Psalms: Volume 1 (Westminster Press, 1982), 95.

[223] See, for example, MacArthur, 114.

[224] Olsen, 43.

[225] Ibid., 45.

[226] Ibid., 49, 42.

[227] Ibid., 49.

[228] Ibid.

[229] Ibid., 50.

[230] Ibid., 348.

[231] Ibid.

Made in the USA
Columbia, SC
24 November 2021